W9-AGL-123

Charlotte's Table

An Anthology of Writings by the 42nd Street Irregulars

Piecemeal Publications
Minneapolis, Minnesota
2004

Published by Piecemeal Publications
Minneapolis, Minnesota

ISBN 0-9747495-0-8

Design, Layout, Editing, Printing
Rick Fournier ♦ Roger S. Jones ♦ Vernelle Kurak

Printed in the United States of America

Contents

Foreword

This book presents a selection of works by a group of writers, called The 42nd Street Irregulars. Based in Minneapolis since 1986, the group has provided its members with support, criticisms, in-group writing activities and weekend workshops, which have allowed them to indulge and celebrate their passion while growing in skill and confidence. These are some of their accomplishments.

Robert K. Anderson

For nearly 20 years Robert K. Anderson was a professional speechwriter and news writer in Minnesota state government before retiring early due to blindness. For the past fifteen years he has been exploring his own creative writing. Poems and essays have appeared in *Evergreen Chronicles*, *Kumquat Meringue*, *ArtWord Quarterly*, *Blue Skunk Companion*, *View from the Loft* and *Men Talk*. He was a winner of the 1996 Loft-McKnight creative nonfiction competition, and in 1999 he was named a S.A.S.E./Jerome Foundation fellow.

Cutting an Orange on Earth Day 1990

It is Sunday morning and I am preparing my breakfast with my usual lack of ceremony. Unwashed, unshaven, standing naked on a floor that sticks to the soles of my feet, I balance a cup and saucer on a nearby glass to clear a tiny space in the clutter on the counter, just large enough to hold an orange.

It amuses me that I, the son of a man whose life is hedged about with reassuring routines, observe so few myself. I live in a clearing in the chaos. Often I eat out of a saucepan or refrigerator dish, frequently while hunched over the sink, to minimize effort or clean-up. "Just get the job done"—that's my motto.

I turn on the Sunday Morning show on CBS to find a feature on the twentieth anniversary of Earth Day. So this morning I decide to eat in a crouch in front of the TV. That's as close as I come to ceremony on Sunday morning.

I remember how Dad couldn't go to bed without first eating his ritual dish of ice cream. He had to be in his pajamas, in his favorite chair, in the living room; the order was all. One night Mom had the women over for bridge and they stayed late. He couldn't follow his routine and it drove him nuts. Since retirement, his morning ritual has become so elaborate it requires preparation the night before. He sections half a grapefruit and half an orange, dishes up exactly three prunes and twenty grapes, and decocts into a shot glass the next day's assortment of pills and vitamins. He lays out his place at the table with all the reverence of a priest preparing the altar. I sometimes wonder if, by the time of his death, his life will have been transmuted entirely into ritual. I, on the other hand, will be taken by surprise, caught in mid-chomp, my feet stuck to the floor in some inopportune corner of my kitchen.

I reach into the fridge for an orange. It's the last one and it looks unpromising. It's flat and dark in spots with wrinkled, leathery skin. I set it on the counter, move a glass to give myself just enough room to maneuver the knife, and begin the cut quarters. This part I'm careful about. I like to cut right on the axis so I get two perfect halves, each divided down the middle by a white cord of membrane, which then becomes my chalk line for the cut into quarters.

I'm going blind and have extreme tunnel vision. Making sense of what I see is a little like trying to piece together a jigsaw puzzle glimpsed in snatches through a keyhole. At this distance, as I hover close to the counter, the orange nearly fills my field of vision. I grasp it firmly with thumb and forefinger near the stem and navel as a guide for my knife. But this morning I'm a little off. I've cut on the bias, and the fruit falls open in a shaft of sunlight revealing not the tidy hemispheres of my intention but something accidental and surpassingly beautiful. The halves are moist and gleaming in the bright morning light. They look kaleidoscopic, marbleized with the membrane distributed over the surface in a random pattern, much like the clouds that wreathe planet Earth. The orange does not reflect the light. It contains it, spills it forth like the sweet, sharp perfume that now pervades the air.

Transfixed, I stare at the world of abundance delivered to me from this taut, tough globe. I think of the Earth itself, glimmering like a prize marble in a game of great stakes, radiant in the dull, dark universe. This orange, in all its freshness, contains within itself the Sun; the rains; the dark, pungent earth; all the cycles of the seasons; everything that gave it being; the very mystery of Creation itself. What a precious jewel, this and its parent jewel, that other thin-skinned globe that hides a heart of fire. How do I know this beauty, how behold it? Is the only way for me to cut it with a knife, to sear the dark fabric of space with a fiery rocket trail? And in knowing it, subjecting it to the compass of my mind and will, do I inevitably destroy it, do I destroy all beauty? I remember Erich Fromm writing that there is only one way of knowing something completely without destroying it, and that is love. How do I love this orange, how do I love this Earth?

I behold, I am transfixed, then I eat. I rip the tender flesh from the skin with my dog-like teeth, incisors sharp from an ancestry of rending flesh. I remember how, as a child, I would slip the skin of the orange section across my teeth, just under my lips, a demonic smile fixed in triumph for all the world to see. I, victor, wear the flesh of the vanquished. But there are no orange smiles on this Earth Day morning.

Suddenly, though not a religious man, and oddly uncomfortable with those who like to talk about their spirituality, I understand why people pray at mealtime. I understand my father's almost compulsive consecration of the commonplace details of everyday life. I understand his pilgrimage every

11

afternoon at five o'clock as he walks widdershins round the back yard filling eleven feeding stations with seed, cracked corn, peanuts and crackers spread with peanut butter for the hordes of squirrels, rabbits, ducks and other birds who wait expectantly, crouched just beyond the bushes or perched on low-hanging branches.

Prayer and ritual are gestures of humility. They are expressions of our peculiar position in creation, acknowledgment that we humans have the power to destroy in knowing, and that we are, despite our dominion, one with the vanquished. Ritual is more than a comforting formality. It is an act of reverence, an entrance into the mystery of the moment. Prayer at mealtime is more than a gesture of thanks for the bounty of this Earth, given to us prodigals who squander our birthright. It is testimony to the sacrament of eating the flesh of our parent, contrite confession that we are, despite our great yearning, only imperfect lovers.

Oh, I love you, my beautiful orange, my beautiful Earth. Teach me, through your beauty, to love more perfectly.

From Blind in the City of Light
(Excerpt from an essay describing a visit to the Louvre
during a trip to Paris)

Bittersweet, this mix of seeing and not-seeing. A lot of
hard work and frustration. I straddle an awkward middle
world, still in love with seeing, unable to surrender to the
order and clarity of pure blackness. My great temptation is
details. I've got to find them first, of course, in the haystack
of the world. Then I stitch them together, my precious fragments, till a face, a gesture, an architectural feature, some
remnant of the visible world I once knew and loved so well,
emerges. No vista or landscape, no broad sweep of sea or
sky. Only a vestige remains of that vibrant, shimmering
world that is forever slipping away from me, but that still
has the power, in the astonishment of a chance detail, to take
my breath away.

Down another corridor, at the top of a flight of stairs,
with sufficient light for me to discern its identity, I saw the
Winged Victory raised high in its place of honor. Could the
artist really have etched out of stone that incredibly delicate
tracery of drapery that swirled so freely over the form, giving the hidden mass shape and substance while at the same
time almost dematerializing it, creating at once the illusion
of flight... the truth of transfiguration? But was I seeing or
merely remembering? Hadn't I thought and felt all this
many years before, after seeing a remarkable photograph in
Time magazine?

The halls of the Louvre were long and high, airy even in
the half-gloom of museum light. I wondered what they did

with all this space when the palace was inhabited. The only thing that justified such a layout was innumerable processions and parades of royalty and their retinue, display and more display of pomp and power. And what of all that space above? I imagined kings, queens, courtiers and courtesans suspended on skyhooks, flying overhead, wave after wave, like flocks of migrating cranes, their great bug-infested wigs and the women with their nether parts swathed in huge balloons of oniony layers of silk and taffeta fanning breezes in the stuffy corridors below.

Then I saw it—out of the corner of my eye, so to speak. Down a long hallway, perhaps fifty yards ahead, gleamed a white form caught in the light that streamed in from a tall narrow window to the left. I recognized it instantly, not so much from details, which I couldn't see at this distance, as from attitude, the signature of the piece—that gesture of melting despair, that curious, sinuous suspension between anguish and languor.

It was Michelangelo's *Dying Slave*. I had loved it from the first time I had seen it—in E.H. Gombrich's *The Story of Art*, the text for Art History 101, upper left corner of a left-hand page. I practically ran toward it, flying over the smooth stone floor, swishing my white cane in front of me with broad, sweeping strokes as the form grew larger and more distinct, its muscles, the agony etched in its face, the ease of death creeping over its limbs, coming into sharper and sharper focus. Then, as I got near enough to see details, it disintegrated. I couldn't keep it in focus. My residual vision was wiped out by the strain of seeing, by the brilliance of the surrounding light, and the figure, and all its power and beauty, vanished.

But for a moment, I had seen it. Not recollected it, not assembled or conjured it, but really seen the thing itself in all its glory. It had entered me directly, impressed itself in its entirety upon my soul. Something that had previously existed only as a flat plane, in shades of grey, had come thrillingly to life.

The power of the eyes. For good reason they are called the windows of the soul. We see into them, and through them, into the heart, the very life of things. We register life whole and radiant, and all its beauty and pity are impressed upon us in one all-encompassing act, shaping us as surely as Michelangelo sculpted his marble. In seeing, we know, we capture the thing, take it into ourselves, are ravished.

What I hated most about blindness was not the practical problems of navigating, maintaining a household, continuing a job; not the social awkwardness, the potential for isolation; not the extra time and clumsiness, the injuries and danger involved in doing the simplest tasks. All this, with patience, I could bear, and amply compensate for. What I grieved was the loss of beauty. For that there was no compensation. The other senses—smell, hearing, touch and motion—could help me get around the city or my apartment, eat, socialize, identify objects, assist in a variety of practical tasks. But nothing could nourish my soul like my eyes. A beautiful face, a meaningful glance, a touching gesture, a grand sunset—for these there were no substitutes.

Prayer at Poolside

I finish my—eight laps only but up from four when I started some years ago—and I rest at poolside, slightly out of breath, standing in the water at chest level, leaning forward with my elbows resting on the cool tiled ledge.

I am praying. No one who sees me would know this. For months I did not know it. It appears that I am only resting, lost in thought, pausing before getting out of the pool so I don't lose my balance. But this is one of the few times I pray with any regularity or deep sincerity.

I pray—or so I discovered when I first verbalized the unconscious state of being in which I found myself after swimming—for the blessing of water, the blessing of health and vigor, the sheer will that gets me out of the apartment to do something my whole physical being shrinks from: exercise.

I pray, by what seems only a natural extension—a jump I am sometimes thoughtless of making in my other, more formal prayers—for all those who are not strong and healthy and vigorous, who don't have the will, energy or ability to get out of the house and engage water or the world with their body and spirit.

Fresh from the exertion and rhythms of the water, its gentle but exacting discipline, I find this is one of the few times when my prayer really flows, is an easy expression of my whole being, is heartfelt and humble, and naturally moves beyond my own fear and happiness to the welfare of others.

Like the ripples my body makes when it first enters the pool, which radiate from that single point of engagement across the calm surface of the water, my prayer flows out from me in who knows what great arcs from that simple point of concentration.

Besides the grace and freedom of movement the water confers on my sluggish land-locked body, besides that incredible lightness of being, the water bestows a lightness of spirit as well—another baptism in the daily renewal of spirit. Each day, as Luther said, is a new baptism, and for that continual renewal, the grace of opportunity implicit in every moment, I give thanks.

Resonance

I walked into a tree the other night.
There it stood, in the middle of the sidewalk looming
Shoulders-wide, coarse-barked, so tall
it snared stars in its branches.

Relic of a lost grove, it had lived in the neighborhood
longer than there had been a neighborhood.
Even the sidewalk deferred, jutting
gingerly around it.

Not me. Preoccupied, full of my own purposes
sole proprietor of a private universe, I walked
face-first into Reality. It shook me
to the roots.

I stood stunned, the full forward thrust of me
forehead, chest, gut, groin and limbs—mashed
against iron. No give. I fought
to catch the wind snatched by that hammerblow.

She could have been Ygdrasil, rooted deep
in the World Soul. Scratched by her unforgiving roughness
I smelled a long-secreted must, felt
the dust of ages settle on startled skin.

I stepped back, breathed her in, tried
to take full measure of that upward thrust

root, trunk, branch and stars
then abandoned my walk, turned

and headed home, shoulders bowed, sticking
to the straight and narrow
marking the stations of the way, mindful
as any novice acolyte.

Empty in astonishment
I rattled round my house that night, struck
like an iron bell, my body
shook, tolled till dawn the holy hours.

The Poison Tree
After William Blake

My friend, unwary, gave me a slight,
Then another, and a third.
I kept my counsel just for spite
And never said a word.

I counted more, stored them up,
Till stinking like a turd
They more than filled my bitter cup.
I never said a word.

I watched and waited like a cat;
Each kindness he averred,
Dismissed—so slight!—what of that?
I never heard a word.

With clever wiles and evil grin,
You'd think the wound had cured.
Indeed! I seemed to let him in—
I'd spring without a word.

The fool! He thought our bond intact.
This my fury only spurred.
What retribution to exact?
Forgive? No such word.

Was it in a dream it came to me?
My soul was deeply stirred.
In a garden grew a Poison Tree
That bloomed without a word

From me, or God—ah, bright Hell-flower!
By itself, I swear, it lured
My hapless foe to taste its power.
I never said a word.

He plucked its bitter fruit. "Take eat"—
Hee-hee! And now interred
He lies beneath my restless feet.
Never says a word.

My garden goes to waste each year,
But not my tree—absurd!
It's watered fresh with rage and tears.
And God? Haven't heard a word.

Out of Loneliness
For John

When, out of loneliness, the body moves
With brute assault against the soundless deep
That separates two souls, the moment proves
Too great for words. What's left to do but weep?
The silence tolls. Our frantic pawing stops,
As greedy lunge, hungry mouths, hearts that spin
Are stilled, and tender selves, defenses dropped,
Learn the limits of insinuating skin.
No comfort but to creep into his arms,
Take refuge in the rising, falling breath,
Steal from tentative embrace sufficient warmth
To stay the dark's admonishments of death.
Enough. This solace tells. What's left to do
Is seize this generous solitude of two.

The Poet's Kiss
For J. Coggins, Grand Marais, Minnesota, 1996
"In every you we address the eternal you."
—Martin Buber, *I and You*

In leaving the cottage, she plants
a peck on its creamy
plastered wall, caresses the smooth
enameled doorjamb, then leans forward into
a full-bodied kiss, smack!
on its egg-shell finish.

That's how she says goodbye, a gentle,
Slow-spun leaving, as loving
as her blessing on arrival: "Ah, yes"
to lawn, porch and sun-drenched daisies.
Goodbye, hello; hello, goodbye, and everything in between
a benediction on the essential nature of things.

To her, every thing is You...
from the barrel-trunked spruce she can barely
wrap her arms around, its ancient storied bark scarred black
against her pale Irish cheek...
from the tabby who ambled into her life that day
her mother died, its wise countenance
calling her to something... care, honor, reverence?
or just to listen to its grumblings from another world...
to the hard stones worn smooth
by thundering Lake Superior, tossed mosaic on
      cobbled beach,
that she spirited away one afternoon, kept

23

in a cup of lake water to see again and again
their moody brilliance—reds, blues, purples and blacks—
as she sat at the desk in the cottage writing, writing
with this pen, that paper,
words.

They shimmer in her hands, those hard, worn words,
tell us simply what she saw that morning
as she sat on the porch with her coffee and cigarettes—
two spare threads cast silken
into reckless air, dream-catcher for the day's catch,
suddenly caught themselves, kissed
into being
by astonished sun.

You, every thing is You to her.
Her life breathed in, its life
breathed out, in and out, out and in,
one breath, one life.
When she quits the cottage with a kiss,
she takes the water, the worn stones,
and casts them like confetti on the restless waves.
"The Water Spirit wants them," she says.

That night, home again, she sleeps, she dreams
of distant, muscled thunder, vaulted
nave pricked by starlight,
a cool spray
fine against her pale Irish cheek,
she dreams...

Three Praises
After Margaret Atwood

Consider the snowflake, perfection itself.
Six-pointed star, in its fall broken
and mended, melted and fused—
how many times? tumbling in free fall
to earth, its resting place
some blunt spike of sharp-needled black spruce
where, jewel-like, its shards
whisper of the broken light
of heaven.
*

Each body on the massage table
from a distance symmetrical, luminous
in the lamplight
its architecture hinting
of an ideal geometry
inscribed, somewhere I suppose, in a sublime circle.
But here, closer in, in the brutal resolution
of this crazy world
to the more intimate eyes of touch
rough and irregular, no two things
the same, not arms or hands or legs or feet
the skin a rough, cobbled field thrown in heaves
limbs fixed akimbo, scarecrow on a stick.
Irreducible, particular
divisible by nothing but itself
not even the halves of the face matching.

How ghastly when a mirror is put
to the seam invisibly stitched along the meridian
that runs like a fault line down the body
How ghastly.
*

Perfection is the enemy of the good.
Consider the mathematical theorem
glimpsed in a moment's fit
scrawled in broken lines across a board.
Consider the child's scribblings
in chalk on a sidewalk...
hop and skip, jump and fall.
Consider every broken utterance
a raving to be known and heard
every badly told story
with a weak ending.

Writing the Body Celestial
"We must labor to be beautiful."
—W.B. Yeats, *Adam's Curse*

Once in ancient China an emperor saw
a dancer so light on her feet she seemed to float on air
and he decreed, for beauty's sake
women should walk with feet like lotus blossoms, barely
touching earth.

And so, for centuries, mothers bound their
daughters' feet
breaking bones, bending the toes under
for beauty's sake. They heard
the cries at night, the wailing for release.
They glided in, across smooth tiled floors
keeping a perilous balance
comforted them, caressed
the tender, budding feet
loosened, then tightened the bands.

A cult of beauty was born. It grew.
Women wrote about the wonder
of lotus feet. They rewrote
their bodies again and again, and not
for men only. For themselves.
They wrote the body celestial.
Secret insignias were embroidered in satin slippers, passed
from generation to generation, and not all
the missionaries of the West, nor wise rulers

of the modern East, could loose them from their bonds
the sweet mystery
of feet that barely touched the earth.

They ached for beauty.
Is it any wonder, then, that Wang Ping
a girl of nine in Mao's China, in the midst of a revolution
to remold humanity
would take out the ancient straps and jeweled slippers,
        and try
in sweet, shameful secrecy, to bind her budding feet?

Now, for another generation, for beauty's sake
she writes of this ancient way, this time
for a restless culture that, again and again, rewrites
the body
in countless images.
She writes, not with her Mother Tongue, where language
slips too easily across the floors of meaning, but
with a bound tongue
careful of roots and syntax, keeping
a perilous balance.

Wang Ping is the author of *Aching for Beauty: Foot-Binding in Ancient China*

28

Judith Coggins

Hey Jude! Where's your bio?

Who Taught You That, Baby?

Who taught you Chinese checkers
and crimping a pie crust just so and
politely avoiding anyone who said
you should wear the color yellow.

Who taught you bicycle riding,
hula-hooping and all the dandy steps
to the Lindy.

Who taught you your colors, how
to part your hair with a rat-tail comb.

Who taught you that rain is wet,
snow is cold and how to write
your own name in big block letters,
for all the world to see.

Who taught you to pour your own juice,
tie your own shoes and much later,
to wipe your own tears.

Who taught you to say "button" in
three languages and "milk" in four
and "thank you" in one, very clearly.

Who, baby, who?
Louder, baby, louder.
Who?

Trees Want Fire

The growling hungry storm has now passed
left a curved scar of stark and leafless trees
standing along the wilderness hillsides,
like tall stick figures, tilted and bruised.

The trees want fire
they want to be ashes
to be born again as young and graceful
saplings, dancing lightly in the spring breeze.

The debate swirls around them
as if they do not know what they want,
informed others bellow and posture
on the fate of the fallen and leaning trees.

The trees want fire
they want to be ashes
they wait, look skyward,
invite the sizzling touch of the lightning
with their raised empty limbs.

Something ageless in them knows
they have already felt the blessed heat
of extinction and rebirth.

The trees want fire.

Sunday Morning 2:00 A.M.

The lake is asleep
moving now and then, shifting
resettling annoyed by the feathery
wind ruffling its surface
like a moth softly whirring
around your head after you
turn out the light.
The waves slap against the shore sand.
All the people in this place
are asleep.

In the hallway, the silence
the soft stillness of rooms
where pillows are warmed by the heads
that rest on them.
The quiet found only
in rural darkness.

Silence is now a part of everyone here
peace surrounds them
keeps them safe
keeps them warm in their long beds
blessed sleep that refreshes and pleases.

They are deep in dreams now
I am here awake.
I tell myself their stories,

speak their prayers slowly
keep their peace
leave them in their dreams.

Examination of Contents
I.   Car—Glove Box

I have lost something. I am looking for it. Three ice scrapers for the windows in winter. I used a credit card once after a storm and ruined it: someone from the New York office called me and accused me of fraud. Not easy to explain why the edge was bent in a peculiar rounded way that made the card reader machine anxious. New Yorkers don't scrape their car windows after a winter storm.

Two cemetery maps: one lists the location and plot number of my older brother's grave at Fort Snelling National Cemetery, the other shows the grave of my friend Tom who is also buried there. Tom's map has a smear of chocolate malt on it. I took a chocolate malt to his graveside once and sat on the summer grass as I ate it. He loved chocolate malts.

I have lost something. I am looking for it.

A small cotton pillow about the size of an eyeglass case filled with herbs that makes the glove box smell like the handkerchief drawer in the bedroom of my godmother Mary Leehy.

A white toothbrush that I found under my windshield wiper after a concert.

A plastic spoon for an A&W drive-in on the main street of my hometown that has now been replaced by a freeway.

Seven books of matches from assorted restaurants between here and Madison, Wisconsin.

A quarter, a dime and 3 pennies that the car wash guys found when they cleaned the inside of the car several summers ago and deposited on the dashboard, banking their honesty.

Copies of insurance and car registrations, encased in small zipped plastic bags.

I have lost something. I am still looking for it.

The Constant Warrior

Medicine Eagle, the Montana Crow Indian
calls in the early morning
while I am tending my flower garden.
The dark birds are quiet on the lawn.
She has dreamt of our old friend Tom, seen
him lion-proud and sunlit, smiling
in the company of two young warriors.

She wonders if he is restless where he is,
chiding us for not keeping him
on the altar of ancestors.
His sense of kinship must be wounded
that we have so little time
to honor his spirit.
She has wakened with the smell of burning
in her nostrils. The forest land to the far west
is in flames. The deep night
has carried the thin sound
of animals screaming.

Only the constant warriors waken
with racing hearts, knowing that death
lies just across the slender doorstep;
there is so little time.
I whisper prayers of safekeeping
across the calm clear liquid
in the yellow watering can, pause

quietly, pouring water over purple petunias,
yellow-smudged violets, bold red geraniums,
the orange hibiscus already dancing
with the morning breeze.

I pour a stream of shimmering drops,
each drop carrying dreams of rain-filled clouds
over western Montana, something
swift and sure to take the fire down,
give her rest, nurture
the weary warrior at her roots.

Dirt Floors

These poems don't amount to much
just some small shelters
I have set up
on the green hillsides of my mind
they're made of bright words and dark words
favorite colors and a found bird feather or two.

Sometimes when I have finished them
I will crawl inside
as if these poems were tents
to check for myself to see they are well-made
tight against the rain and snow
protected from the pillage of an editing pen.
I see it differently
for the first time
from the inside.

See a particular phrase held up
against the daylight
and am comforted by it.
When I'm inside
sitting on the cool dirt floors
almost all my poems have dirt floors
I am still and listening
to see if this poem wanted to tell me something.

The words that form the roof

sometimes shift a bit
in the light breeze
the words whispering
bumping up against each other.

I will hear them
telling me that if I move this word
or shift that one, more sky will show
if I want a patch of sky
a nice thin slice of cobalt or bird egg blue.

Sometimes, I leave the sky out
use words to cover the sky
hide the idea of sky
some poems don't want sky.

Water Myth

The lake has a sandy bottom,
many large pebbles along the beaches
but nothing like this line of boulders
that marks the gradual descent to the deepest water.

There is a leader
dark gray, almost black and large
the width of an old oak tree
ahead of all the others.

The line behind is graceful, slightly curved arc
of others, some large some small
browns and blacks, some speckled almost blue
some smooth
the lake washes over them
shines them all.

La Longe, the French Canadian tells me
in his wavering English
that the old Indians here say it was
a group of Ogalala coming across the lake
late one bitter winter day, overtaken by a snow squall.

They lost their way, died where they fell
men, women, five small children, two dogs.
The dogs, he says, pointing one thin dark finger
toward the last two rocks, kept the wolves away.

Brother Wolf was hungry but not wise.
He came to eat.
He could only sharpen his teeth on the rocks.

Sometimes in the dark and soft murmuring night
when the wind brings a scent of cedar smoke
from the eastern island,
I hear a wolf call
across the clear knowing water.

Why Zebras Have Not Been Domesticated
A Few Caprices for MKV

1.   Zebras are quite content and honored to assist small children in learning the alphabet, using their unusual coloration and design to make memorable the last wonderful letter. The aardvarks have the competitive edge and the ego to go with being first. Zebras are not pushy or rude and think that being unusual and last is very special indeed.

2.   Zebras are accustomed to roaming where they choose, following the seasons across the Serengeti, do not care for traffic lights or turn signals. They prefer the veldt and blue skies overhead, although they do admit to some curiosity about red convertibles.

3.   Zebras have been told of the music of Mozart and Brahms. They are attentive listeners but wonder idly how any sound could compare to the birds' chorus at dawn when a sun-rising breeze ruffles the tree leaves and sweeps along the grass tops. They are, however, somewhat interested in piano keys and feel some thoughtful kinship.

4.   Zebras can spot rainfall on a far horizon and will run sixty miles to drink the fresh water as it fills the lowland gullies. They have never heard of windshield wipers, cannot fathom a reason to keep the rain away from their serious long noble faces.

5.   Zebras travel in herds and often deliberately create movement and excitement, hooves drumming to confuse an attacking predator. The whirl of pattern and dust and noise is a dizzying sight, making it difficult to see where one animal begins and ends. They understand that dancing fast does sometimes dazzle and distract an audience.

6.   Zebras are individual and unique. No two are exactly alike. Their stripes can be used like fingerprints to tell one zebra from another. The foals memorize the pattern of their mothers' stripes. In hotter climates, there are more stripes in the zebra's coat. They are politely astounded that anyone would think that they all look alike. Athletic shoes that cost $200 a pair, they conclude, all look alike. Zebras are not without a sense of humor.

7.   When the zebra herd flees danger, they call to one another with a short barking sound so that no one zebra becomes lost in the confusion. If one of the herd does become lost, the whole herd will search until the lost zebra is found. They are puzzled by the idea that the human species does not take such care over someone who strays away in fear.

8.   Zebras need to drink water daily. To all the African animals, the sight of a herd of zebras grazing always means there is water nearby. The zebras, when told of large billboards and bright neon signs can only marvel with some modesty at their own advertising gimmick. Zebras appreciate irony.

This Heart

From the green front door
I start my winter walk
to school.

I am carrying a box of valentines
across the ice patches and furnace cinders
scattered like gray dust, meant to make walking safer.

My mother stands in the doorway
as I move away from the house, turn
toward the school. She is waving
smiling, calling her "be careful" softly.

The street is empty.
I am late and hurrying
no one looks out on this foggy February morning
no one sees the small child dressed in blue
carrying love, carrying her heart and her mother's heart
across the slippery sidewalks.

I was afraid to let go of the box
to wave goodbye.
I am in the schoolyard when I stumble
at the edge of a puddle in front of me
dropping the white box of valentines
the wind tips it over in the muddy water
valentines tumble out and float quietly away

red hearts waving.

When my mother died many years later
far away in another city
I turned in that direction, to that place
to her somewhere in the night
and waved my arm
moved it back and forth
slowly steadily
I waved to her bright heart
floating away from us.

The Very Nearly Last Snowfall

Standing straight and alone
in the midnight gauze of the
persistent snowfall,
my orange shovel and I rest a moment.

The muffled respiration that is my own breathing,
my neighbor's windchime leaning with some complaint
into the northern gusts, the faint whisper
of the snow falling
are the only sounds.

There are no planes,
no cars or buses
not even a barking dog.
The shovel and I
are both perfectly still.

Everyone else has gone to bed,
gone to work, gone to Florida
gone securely mad, beaten finally
by this last closed fist of winter.

We are here, unappointed but willing
workers doing this singular task,
clearing paths neatly, calmly moving
small loads of snow around
so that if anyone wakens,

comes home or at the last minute,
bravely dares to seek sanity again,
they will know we were here
and that a way into warmth, safety
has been cleared for them.
Only for them.

Rick Fournier

Retired in 1991 after teaching high school, college and adult classes for thirty-three years and began writing. Has had five poems published in anthologies, as well as fifty-five others in various magazines and journals. Has self-published three chapbooks of poems and is currently working on a novel about the American West in the 1870's. He is busy drawing and painting pictures, traveling, shooting photographs and thinking how wonderful it is to be able to live such a life.

Tea?

For the first time in her life Susan had a secret, a real secret; something that no one else knew about. She savored it, just as she did the strawberries that she and her cousin Sheila found that morning under the pine trees between the cabins of the resort where they were staying. The berries were so tiny that at first the girls could hardly see them, but once they became better at spotting the dots of red amongst the pine needles they gathered about a half cup each. Neither Susan nor Sheila had admitted to the other that picking the berries would put them in a position to see whatever was going on at the cabin next door, yet each of them stole regular glances at it.

Two rangers had visited the cabin early that morning accompanied by the resort manager who stood off to one side and shifted from foot to foot while the rangers talked to the young man who had moved in the previous afternoon. Susan had been the only one from her cabin who had seen the man arrive with a young woman in a red sports sedan the evening before. She had been impressed by the car, their good looks, their stylish clothes and their leather-trimmed canvas luggage, all of which matched.

The rangers arrived shortly after Susan and Sheila woke up and they watched, peering out from their bunks, one looking over the curtain and one looking under. The young man was wearing a cast on his leg and leaning on a cane when he came out to talk to the rangers. This puzzled Susan. Then the young man invited the rangers into his cabin. The girls had heard nothing of what was being said, yet they knew something was going on by the serious faces of the rangers and from interesting gestures that they made. This morning the red car was nowhere to be seen.

To keep up their watch on the cabin the girls put off going in to breakfast as long as they could, but when Susan's mother finally said, "You can eat now, or you can go without," they bolted away from their posts and hurriedly dressed. While they were doing the dishes the girls saw the rangers walk to their pickup and drive away. They were disappointed; excitement was their specialty, and their keen eyes their means of achieving it.

As they picked the berries, they knew they would soon be called back into their cabin to discuss what the afternoon outing would be. They hoped the young man next door would come out before that happened. He did not disappoint them.

He appeared to be in his mid-twenties, not much taller than the girls, and had very dark, closely cropped hair. Susan agreed with Sheila's earlier assessment that he was, "handsome enough to be a model or an actor." Leaning on his cane he moved to a chair on the tiny patio in front of his cabin and sat down, putting the leg with the cast on it up on the other chair. Susan noticed that his cast was almost as white as the polo shirt he was wearing and smiled to herself. Something is going on here, she thought. The shorts he wore were a deep red color. On his right foot was a dark leather sandal, but his left foot which stuck out just below the cast was bare. The cast encased his leg upward to just below the knee and there was a metal rung for him to step on under the foot.

Susan, at fourteen, was six months older than Sheila, her cousin, and just slightly taller. They had been alternating going on vacations with one another's families for as long as they could remember, and on a few occasions both families had gone together. Over the years both girls had grown tall and slim, with upper bodies that were trying to catch up with their long legs. They usually spent their vacation days in shorts and lightweight, loose sweatshirts that had their makers' names emblazoned on the fronts or the backs.

They usually wore sneakers or sandals on their feet and made sure that their legs got properly tan enough to be set off by the carefully chosen colors of their shorts. They both favored black shorts, but of course they would never wear them on the same day. Susan thought of her own hair as dark blond and described Sheila's hair as "auburn." Sheila claimed she was a brunette. Both girls agreed that their mothers, who were sisters, were hopelessly out of date since neither would allow them to dye or even tint their hair.

The vacation trips usually took them to some state or national park in the United States, but this year they had traveled all the way to Jasper National Park in Alberta, Canada, in the family van that Susan's father had bought that spring and was very proud of. The park was farther than either girl, or their parents, had ever been from home.

Sheila had enjoyed writing out the full name of the park on the postcards that she was sending to friends in the small Wisconsin town she lived in. Susan didn't bother with postcards anymore. "What's the use," she said to Sheila and to her mother, "I always get home before the cards do." Besides, her friends back home in Chicago were no longer impressed by vacation postcards.

"What are you picking?"

Susan was startled, speechless. She simply stared at the young man, never thinking he might speak to them.

"Strawberries," Sheila finally said.

"Are there really wild strawberries there? I can't see them from here." His voice was smooth, cultivated. Susan thought, maybe he's from the East someplace, like Boston. Maybe he was from England even! Without thinking and still unable to speak, Susan surprised herself by walking over and holding out her hand to him showing the berries she had gathered. He looked up at her. "Do you mind if I taste one?" he asked. Susan shook her head. Taking his eyes from hers for only a moment he carefully reached out and took one of the tiny berries, his fingers just brushing the palm of her hand. He put the berry into his mouth, leaned back for a moment closing his eyes and said, "Umm, nothing tastes as utterly wonderful as a wild strawberry, thank you."

"Have more," Susan, finally was able to say. But he just looked at her, smiled and shook his head.

"No, you eat them, or save them for your family. Thank you for sharing, I really appreciate it." Susan wanted to stay, to look at him, to listen to him. Yet at the same time, she wanted to turn and run. She wanted to talk to him, to ask him things, like where was the car, and where was the young woman who was with him last night, and why had the rangers been there earlier? She was even willing to settle for just standing there in his gaze, but at that moment her father came to the door of their cabin to call them in. Both girls turned quickly after saying "Bye."

On the way to their cabin they grinned at each other. "Utterly wonderful," thought Susan; she had never heard anyone talk like that.

As the girls walked over to their cabin, which was just like all the others in the row, Susan saw that her father was still in his undershirt. She had been trying for years to get him to wear t-shirts with a pocket, or at least colored undershirts that didn't look so much like underwear, but he was unwilling to make a change from either the undershirts or the baggy pants and faded flannel shirts he liked when he was around the house or on vacation. Susan felt that the clothes he wore made him look a little old and pot-bellied. He had also quit shaving, which he always did on vacation, so his face was covered by a five-day stubble.

Why is he such a slob around us? Susan asked herself. When he went to work in his police sergeant uniform at home in Chicago he always looked quite sharp. Susan's dad was aware of her feelings about his appearance and that morning when she and Sheila had come in for breakfast, he looked up from his sports magazine and said, "Ah, the princesses have come from the castle to dine with the peasants."

It was one of his favorite lines and always made Susan wince, but he always got a little laugh and a mock bow from Sheila. "Don't encourage him," said Susan.

The sore throat Susan complained of shortly after breakfast was not altogether a fabrication, but its intensity certainly had grown into a work of fiction by the time they came in to talk over the day's excursion. It led to her mother's usual reaction, a hand on the forehead and the statement, "You do seem a bit warm," followed by, "Take two aspirins and lie down for a little while." This Susan dutifully did. When it was time to leave for their hike in the Maligne Canyon it was with great reluctance that Susan's parents let her stay at the cabin by herself rather than go along.

When no one else was looking, Sheila rolled her eyes at Susan and stuck out her tongue to let her know that she was not fooled. Then, after instructions on the opening and heating up of the package of dry chicken soup, they were gone. Susan watched the van pull away and sat back in a chair to enjoy the "utterly delicious" feeling of being alone and in charge of whatever this part of the day would bring.

Susan read a magazine article and then puttered around the cabin for awhile not allowing herself a look to see if he was still on the patio. Finally she went to the window. Yes, there he was. Simply sitting and staring into space. Suddenly a helicopter flew over quite low with a loud chopping sound and he looked up at it. Susan debated about what she should do. Her parents, of course, would expect her to stay in the cabin, but what would be wrong with walking over to the lodge to get a can of pop out of the machine. It would take her right past him in both directions and the thought gave her a small chill. Who is he? she wondered, and what is he up to?

Susan sat down and looked at the Jasper Park brochure which listed all of the activities in the area. She opened to the Maligne Canyon section and read about the self-guiding trail to which the rest of the family had gone, about how the river plunged 23 meters in the steep canyon and the notes on the need for caution. She felt a little left out, not being with them, but then decided it was OK. She wanted to learn what was going on and this was the only way see could do so.

Without giving herself time to change her mind, Susan went into her room, grabbed her small flat leather handbag and walked out the door. Looking neither right nor left she walked along the sidewalk briskly. She would maintain a certain distance, she thought, just greet him if he said anything and then continue. Susan's resolve melted instantly when he looked up and saw her coming and smiled at her.

"Did your family enjoy the berries?" he asked, in a cheerful voice.

Susan slowed. "Uh, no, not yet. We'll eat them later."

"Don't let them stand around and lose their flavor, they're very delicate you know."

"All right, we won't." Susan had stopped, but started to move on.

Then he said, "I wonder if I might impose on you and ask a very great favor." Susan hesitated. "It's quite awkward for me to move around, and I wondered if you would put the tea kettle on for me. I'd like to make some tea, but I have a very hard time lighting the stove since it requires a match."

Suddenly Susan was torn. She could hear her mother saying that she should never go into a stranger's house, especially if that stranger was a man. But she could also hear her mother saying that when disabled people need our help, we should give it to them. And, of course, here was a perfect chance to learn what was going on, just what she wanted-- or thought she wanted. Now she wasn't so sure.

"I suppose I can handle making the tea, but I must say that stove has totally thwarted me."

"Sure," said Susan, startled at her agreement.

"My name is Stewart, and you are. . .?

"I'm Susan."

"The other girl?"

"She's my cousin Sheila."

"What lovely names, Susan and Sheila. Well Susan, I really appreciate your helping me out."

Susan smiled and nodded and walked past him to the door of the cabin. When he made no move to indicate that he would follow she felt relieved.

Once inside the cabin Susan saw that some of the luggage that she had admired the previous evening still stood in the small living room. She turned into the kitchen and found an elegant wooden box with brass fittings, like a small theater trunk, on the table.

"Open that little trunk, Susan," called Stewart, "and you'll find the teakettle."

Susan undid the latch and lifted the two sections of the trunk a little so they could swing away from one another. Sure enough, in various indented sections was an entire tea set with a stainless steel teakettle near the bottom. The other sections held the white China teapot, cups, saucers, cream pitcher, sugar bowl, and the extra water pot. It was as complete as the tiny tea set that Susan had owned and loved as a child.

Across the top on each side of the chest were small tins of tea, each having a different brilliant color and each an exotic name. Susan had no idea there were so many different kinds of tea. At her house, tea bags simply came out of a box from the supermarket. Susan was allowed to drink tea, though coffee was forbidden.

"This is just like the tea set I had when I was a little girl," Susan called through the door, as she got out the teakettle and filled it with water from the tap.

"Yes, that's what everyone says. Isn't it delightful? It was a gift from my wife's grandmother. She lives in England. You know, they take their tea quite seriously there."

It took Susan two tries to light the stove, since she dropped the match and turned the burner off when the flame leaped up and startled her the first time. Then she put the filled teakettle on the flame and slowly removed the teapot from its nest.

"You'll see there's a metal tea ball by the stove that the tea goes into," the young man called. Susan looked through the window at him, a little surprised that he would assume that she would make the tea. Would he ask her to share it, she wondered.

"Which kind would you like?" Susan asked.

"What's your favorite?"

"I don't drink tea very often, usually pop."

"Then let's have the Jasmine, I think you'd like that."

Susan froze; he was getting ahead of her. He was going to ask her to stay. Well, what if he did? she thought, we'll be on the patio, outside, in sight of everyone. Her secret hung just on the edge of her awareness, but she brushed it aside. It will be OK she thought, as she took out the small yellow tin of tea marked with flowing script.

"How much tea do I put in?"

"About a teaspoon should do. By the way, on the counter there is a red metal plaid-colored box, do you see it?" Susan looked and found the box. The painted label said it was Scottish shortbread. "Put it on the tray when you bring it. I think you'll find them delightful."

He did assume she was going to stay. Susan wondered what she should do. As before, part of her wanted to flee. There were just too many unanswered questions. The other part of her wanted to stay and enjoy this mysterious stranger, and this kind of situation she had never known before. He seemed so gentle in his voice and manner, yet he seemed to take control in the way he took things for granted.

Susan stiffened. He knew her family was gone, she thought, he would have seen them leave. He knew she had stayed behind; he knew that she had not only remained behind but that she had deliberately walked past his cabin.

Now she was in his cabin and no one else was there. Where was the young woman? Susan thought as she put the tea into the tea ball. It seemed that he was reading her thoughts.

"Susan, did you see that the rangers were here this morning?"

"Yes, I saw them."

His voice was serious. "They're looking for my wife. She disappeared last night about five and hasn't returned. They came to tell me how things are going in their search."

Susan stood inside the screen door. "That's terrible, do they have any idea...?"

"They found her car in that canyon north of here, near one of the bridges. I think it's called the Maligne River. It's not very far from here. She went out to take some photographs in the evening light. She's a good photographer. Takes a lot of pictures."

"That's where my family went to go hiking this morning."

"They won't get into the canyon. The rangers said they closed the area so their search with dogs won't be disturbed."

Susan stared through the screen at him. He seemed very far away. "That helicopter that went over earlier is also looking for her," he said. "They think she may have fallen...somewhere." His voice was quiet and distant. "I'm hoping they find her, but still we should have tea, don't you think?"

"Yes, I suppose so," said Susan. She turned back and started putting cups and saucers on the tray. A picture of a woman falling helplessly down a cliff and into a river came into her mind. The kettle began to whistle and Susan turned off the flame.

"I suppose a girl as pretty as you is bound to have a boyfriend."

Susan pictured Arnold Bayless, his angular body, acne and Adam's apple.

"I have a boy whose a friend, but not really a boyfriend."

"You'll have lots of them, I'm sure."

Susan wondered if he planned to continue discussing her non-existent love-life.

"Susan!" His voice was not loud, but sharp and firm and it startled her. She stepped to the inside of the screen door. "Listen, just let everything go. You should go back to your cabin." Susan hesitated. "Right now, I think." Susan opened the door wondering what was happening. Stewart was still sitting in the same place and nothing seemed different.

"What's the matter?"

"I'm sorry, but you should be on your way. We'll have our tea some other time, perhaps." He was looking at her. "Say listen, take the shortbread, the plaid box, take it with you. Please, I want you to have it. You can share them with your cousin."

He turned to look at the office of the lodge and following his gaze Susan saw that a number of cars were pulling up, including the ranger pickup. She reached over and picked up her purse, hesitated for a moment and then also picked up the plaid box and walked out onto the small patio. Stewart smiled at her and nodded, pleased that she had taken the box. Susan had no idea what to say. Something was happening and she knew she had to leave, but no words came to her.

"I guess I'll find out what happened now, don't you think?" Stewart said slowly and evenly. Susan nodded. "Susan, don't think badly of me, and thank you for trying to help." He held out his hand and she took it. Then he looked away. "You'd better go. It's been a great pleasure to meet you." His voice was very serious.

After walking back to the cabin, Susan tucked the plaid box under her pillow, and then went into the kitchen to watch out the window. From her father's explanations Susan knew that the officers in the light blue uniforms were from the province and those in the dark blue were the mounties. The rangers, of course, wore green uniforms. Susan wondered why there were so many different officers talking to Stewart. Then another police car pulled up into Stewart's driveway from the town of Jasper, and officers in tan uniforms got out and walked over to the group.

Soon they were helping Stewart rise from his chair and walk slowly over to their car and get in. The other officers were going into his cabin and coming out with various items in plastic bags. In the Jasper police car, the provincial officer was talking to Stewart while another officer was putting up a long yellow plastic strip mounted on thin rods around the cabin which said "Police line—do not cross," over and over again. Then the officers from the various agencies stood around and talked to each other and to the manager and his wife for what seemed like forever. Susan longed to hear what they were saying, but she didn't dare go out.

Suddenly the door of the cabin burst open and Susan's mother came in. With her attention on the cabin next door Susan had not even heard the car pull in. "Thank goodness, you're OK," said Susan's mother. Sheila was right behind her and she looked at Susan with amazement.

"Why? What's the matter?"

Her mother held her arms and looked at her. "That man next door, the police think he may have pushed his wife off a cliff and into the river."

Susan looked outside and saw that the police car with Stewart in the back seat was still there. Her mother came and stood beside her at the window.

"How do you know that?"

"Well, don't be upset. You know how your father is when it comes to finding out what's going on. They wouldn't let us into the canyon because they were searching for the woman, his wife, but, of course, Dad gets his badge out and offers to help and before you know it they're telling him everything."

"They found her," said Sheila, excited. "We were standing with one of the rangers when the call came on his walkie-talkie. They found her with the helicopter and went down to get her. Just like on a TV show."

"See, Dad is over there talking to the mounties now," said Susan's mother. Sure enough, there was her father deep in conversation with one of the mounties. "Probably comparing cases. Policemen are all alike."

While they stood and watched, the car with Stewart in the back seat started to pull away. Inside, Susan felt like her stomach was a paper bag that was slowly crumpling up. She wasn't sure if she was feeling sad or angry or frightened. Perhaps it was all of them. She chewed on her lower lip and tried not to cry. Maybe that's what he meant when he said, "Don't think badly of me."

Susan saw her dad turn from the officer he had been talking to and walk toward their cabin. Now we'll know, she thought.

As he entered, he shook his head and said, "Oh boy, that is some amateur bluebeard we got next door."

"Is bluebeard the guy who killed his wives?" asked Susan's mother.

"You know it. Looks like this guy tried to start doing the same thing, but he didn't get very far. He thinks he's pretty slick, let me tell you."

"What do you mean?"

"Well, first of all, that's no broken leg, It's a fake!"

Susan stared at her father. She knew that! How had they found out, she wondered.

"He never got out of the car when they checked in yesterday so no one knew," her father continued.

I knew! thought Susan, I knew!

"Last night, they crossed one of the bridges and went up the canyon together, according to the mounties. Then he apparently did the dirty deed, left the car and hiked back here as it was getting dark. He put the cast on his leg after he got back here."

"But why?" asked Sheila.

"Why? So it would look like it would be impossible for him to be out walking back here. But they got his boots now and they're out there making plaster casts of his tracks. He's so dumb that they found the wrappers from the rolls of cast-making stuff in the dumpster right off the bat. Oh, they got this guy good."

"What makes them think he pushed her?" asked Sheila.

"She's got bruises on her back, for one thing, where he slammed her. See, the car is locked, she's in the river, the key is in her pocket. He's back here with a leg in a cast. Hey, it looks perfect, right? How could he have anything to do with it?"

Susan's dad was into his favorite role: telling about the latest case with all of the embellishments of a good story-teller.

"There's just one other little thing this bucko hasn't counted on."

"What's that?"

"He thinks she's dead. He thinks she drowned in the river, or hit her head," her dad said and laughed.

"She's still alive?" asked Susan.

"That's right," he said cheerfully. "The one thing our boy didn't figure on. Hey, she's in rough shape, the mounties tell me. She damn near drowned, and then exposure, you know, wet and cold. But she made it to an island and managed to get through the night. By now she's in the hospital. She must be some tough gal. Oh man, those guys aren't going to tell him what they know. They'll just let him tell his story, and then they will nail him! God, I'd love to be there."

"But why would he do that? Why would he try to kill her?" asked Susan, wondering how someone so nice could be dangerous.

"Probably a rich family that didn't want her to marry him. Maybe big life insurance settlement too," Susan's dad replied. "The mounties have been in contact with her family since last night. The family insisted on bringing in the helicopter, even if they had to pay for it. Some of them are on their way out here now. That guy is going to do life, you better believe it."

Susan's dad sounded satisfied. He liked "clean convictions," as he often told them.

Susan's mother asked, "How did he know how to make a cast for his leg?"

"The family told the mounties he had worked as an orderly and was being trained as a medic in a hospital."

Then her mother had her hand on Susan's forehead again. "You look pale, honey, maybe you should go lie down for a bit. How's the throat?"

"Oh, it still hurts a little, but not bad," said Susan, as she turned to walk into the bedroom, "but maybe you're right." She caught Sheila's eye as she left the room and Sheila followed her, closing the door behind them.

"Well. What happened?" Sheila asked, excited.

Susan held her finger up to her lips and turned to her bunk. Slowly she lifted the pillow to show the plaid box of cookies. Sheila's eyes widened. "Susan! Are they from . . .?"

Susan nodded slowly still feeling a little quivery inside. "We almost had tea together."

"Oh, wow. Tell me, tell me, tell me!"

But before Susan could say anything her mother swung open the door and asked, "Would either of you like a nice hot cup of tea, or some pop? We could get out some cookies and eat the berries you picked."

The girls looked at each other and then smiled and nodded. Tea, they agreed, would be just the thing.

Roger S. Jones

After 32 years in the Department of Physics of the University of Minnesota, during which time Roger published two popular books on physics, *Physics as Metaphor* and *Physics for the Rest of Us*, he retired in 1999 to do, among other things, some creative writing in other areas. Since then, one of his short stories was published in the *Christian Science Monitor*, and an essay won a prize in the St. Paul Capital New Year contest.

Sisters

Why did I call her Mrs. Darling, while her elder sister I always knew as Katie? She lived in the apartment two flights above us, one of the retinue of close friends with whom Mom maintained daily and intimate contact in our Washington Heights neighborhood of the 1940s. It was a kind of local clan, second in importance only to our family. Mrs. Darling and another friend, Mrs. Fleischman, often came to our apartment in the evening to play pinochle for pennies with my parents. They would bicker over the hands. Dad was always blaming Mom or the other women for ruining his chances of winning. They usually humored him.

I barely remember Mr. Darling—a tall, fair, soft-spoken man who had widowed Esther Darling some years earlier. To Mom she was always Tessie, forcing me to deal with a profusion of names, as bad as a Russian novel. To make matters worse, Mrs. Darling always called me and others in her circle of affection, "darling," and I often wondered whether this reflected some unique privilege attached to her name.

Katie Rhineman, herself recently widowed, came to live with her sister in our building. She was several years older than Mrs. Darling—in her seventies—round, wrinkled, white-haired, and jovial, but savvy and sharp-tongued. Mom and I had visited Katie once in her dilapidated apartment in Harlem. She took us shopping in the local food market, housed beneath the elevated subway at 125th Street. It was a noisy cavernous space of pungent smells and the colorful wares of endless stalls. Merchants plied us with an amazing variety of squirming fish, bloody meat, and farm-fresh vegetables, not to mention exotic trinkets and clothes, such as I'd never seen or imagined—and all under one roof. Katie bargained and haggled her way from stall to stall, until she acquired the ingredients for the wonderful fish dinner she would later cook for us. I marveled at the splendor she conjured amidst all the squalor.

The sisters didn't get along well at all. They fought and picked on each other constantly. I had never known that sweet kindly Mrs. Darling had such a mean streak. "That Katie—she never lifts a finger. I'm supposed to wait on her hand and foot. One of these days I'll throw her out and good riddance." They took turns sitting in our kitchen, using Mom as a sounding board for their complaints and exasperations. "If she vasn't mine sister," Katie would say, "I vouldn't talk to her—vich I don't anyvays." Mom always sympathized and tried to help, but they were basically incompatible. Only blood enabled them to remain within firing distance of each other.

Whenever she had an electrical or repair problem, Mrs. Darling would call on me, the great engineer on the ground floor, and I would sneak Dad's tool box upstairs to the rescue. I would replace an electrical plug or tighten a door hinge, and Mrs. Darling would tell me how resourceful and clever I was and reward me with milk and cookies. And I loved to listen to the magnificent radio in its large polished-wood cabinet that stood proudly on the floor of her living room. We had a console radio too, but not nearly as imposing as Mrs. Darling's with its gleaming dial, centered on an eerie green "eye" that winked and flashed with changes in the reception, and with a loudspeaker that brought the announcers and performers to life right there in the room.

The radio was usually tuned to WEVD, the most famous of the local New York Jewish stations. I was always attracted to its exotic music and the flamboyant but mysterious language, whose meaning I could only guess at between the occasional interruptions—half in English and half in Yiddish—for station breaks and commercials. "Try Finkelstein's kosher salami. It's a *mechaieh!*" The allure and freedom of Mrs. Darling's rooms were always a welcome relief from our more austere apartment, where I had little privacy and was often under the disapproving eye of my father. That haven up the stairs was my rich reward for doing some small task or favor for Mrs. Darling.

But there was one job I couldn't handle. The great shame of Mrs. Darling's life was that she couldn't read. Her sad lamentations prompted me, the brilliant ten-year-old student, to try tutoring her. She resisted at first. She knew her limitations, but ultimately her soft heart gave in to my confident boasts.

We held class in her kitchen once or twice a week. I brought her picture books with large lettering, and I leaned on her ability to read the numbers 1 through 10 and the letters A, K, Q and J on playing cards. For weeks, we struggled again and again through the same words and simple sentences. But somehow she never seemed to get the knack. It was a noble but hopeless effort. Katie, who could read no better but didn't care, chuckled and clucked in the background over her sister's failure and stupidity. "Vot a lummox!"

"Aaah shut up," Mrs. Darling would yell back at Katie. "You can't even count in English." "*Gae cockin!*" was Katie's classic Yiddish retort. But Mrs. Darling was touched and flattered by my efforts, and she paid me back in spades with milk, cake and candy, while sticking her tongue out at her sister.

Katie was a wonderful baker. She was famous for her *bulkes*, a large round powdered yeast roll, with a chewy texture and a buttery smell and taste directly from Paradise. She baked them only once or twice a year and always gave some to Mom. But I was insatiable. I would run upstairs to beg Katie for one or two more, which she would slather with butter and feed to me, looking on with her warm smiling eyes. She and Mrs. Darling were so kind and generous to me. I couldn't understand why they were so hateful to each other.

One day Katie turned up with a "boyfriend." Mrs. Darling was fit to be tied. "How did that witch get so lucky?" Ever since Mr. Darling died, she had been on the lookout for a man, but with little luck. She envied Mom and Mrs. Fleischman, who still had their husbands, despite all their faults. Always on her best behavior when Dad was around, she would smile, pay him compliments, and be oh so patronizing and grateful when Dad "corrected" her card playing. She had all but resigned herself to living out her days as a widow in the company of her irritating sister, when Katie dropped her bomb.

Katie's "beau," Mr. Goldman, was a hobbled milquetoast widower in his eighties. He had been in despair after the loss of his dear wife, and Katie was a godsend. She would feed him a good meal and walk with him to his favorite park bench, where they would sit and talk and hold hands. He was smitten with Katie, and Katie wasn't about to look a gift horse in the mouth. Besides, he had a $15,000 nest egg that Katie found out about very soon. It wasn't long before they were engaged. Katie promised always to take care of him, but of course in return she insisted that he change his will in her favor, in effect disinheriting his own children. "Vot did dey ever do for you, like I do for you?" she argued. "Ya ya, dot's right," Mr. Goldman agreed, unwilling to jeopardize his good fortune.

They were married. Six weeks later, Mr. Goldman dropped dead, and Katie inherited the money. The children protested and took Katie to court, but the will was very recent, completely legal and unequivocal. Mr. Goldman had been of sound mind, as far as anyone could tell, and he'd made his choice.

Mrs. Darling was furious. She accused Katie of every dirty scheme in the book, but Katie remained unruffled. "Who else did he have?" she responded calmly. "I vas de one vot took care of him dose last four monts. Me. Me. Not his children. Vy should I give dem anyting? All dey vanted vas his money."

"And you didn't?" stabbed back Mrs. Darling. But it was pointless to argue. Katie held all the trump cards. Mrs. Darling was bitter but resigned. "That old bitch got a man *and* a fortune. She can't read a word, but she got that will changed all right. What the hell! My sister—she should only drop dead!"

Easy Rider
For Bob Anderson

I feel strangely unstable on my bike today—a bit wobbly on the curves and uncommonly aware of balancing. Me, a 29-year veteran of biking the parkways and streets of Minneapolis. Some rare blend of poor sleep, excess heat and softened consciousness has made me hypersensitive to the enveloping world—the flanking shade trees, the irregularities in the road, the sparkling wind-chiseled lake—even the mechanical action of the cranks, the smooth sliding of the freshly lubricated chain, and my own tiny balance adjustments.

I slip into the green tunnel on Lake Harriet's south shore, which focuses and directs my ride. The bike seems to shift into auto pilot. I coast down a knoll into the hot south wind, approaching and then following the north rim of the lake. I don't fight the wind. I accept a moderate speed, riding against—and yet somehow with—the currents of air, supplying just enough pedal pressure to allow the bike, the path and the surroundings to guide me on this benevolent ride. Everything seems new and charmed, as if I had not taken this path a thousand times before.

I near a shirtless skater, swaying left and right in rhythmic oscillations. I call out, "passing...left," in my habitual bike-path etiquette. He eases to the right, maintaining but limiting his horizontal amplitude to give me wide berth. Without looking back, he waves me on, and I return a soft "thank you," as I pass. A couple biking abreast, gently switches into tandem formation at my "passing...left." Bikers and skaters glide by the sails and reeds, weaving and passing on the great Lake Harriet merry-go-round. Ahead, a father on skates hobbles across the grass toward the bike path, leading his little son on a tricycle. He sees me coming and corrects his trajectory to approach on a tangent, reaching the path after me and sparing me from having to call out, "passing...left."

I feel as though I'm in Wagner's *Die Meistersinger* at the great song contest. As each contestant comes forward, the apprentices call out:

Silence, silence

No talking and no murmuring.

But when the hero unexpectedly takes the podium, the crowd is breathless and mute, and the apprentices quip:

All is expectancy; there's not a murmur

So we shall not call out "silence."

In German, murmur—*Gesumm*—and silence—*Silentium* —rhyme, and the music reflects the wry humor of the apprentices. No rhyme or music accompany my silent refrain, but its symmetry seems to complete the harmony of the moment.

On the Parkway now, I freewheel toward 50th, traversing the splashed shadows of the sheltering trees above me. The mottled fluctuating abstractions call up Renoir, and the showering shade soothes and cools me. I speed down the double hills beyond Lyndale. The dancing dappled shadows contrast so starkly with the bright sunlit pavement that I cannot see the cracks and potholes. But my concern dissolves as I allow memory and instinct to guide me, and I revel in the rushing air and effortless speed.

I ride under the 35W overpass. The open space between the north- and southbound lanes casts sharp shadows on the road, whose parallel edges, I observe with delight, are alternately tinged red and blue, demonstrating the uncanny spectral effects that inspired Goethe's radical color theory. Both the sensible and the visionary worlds seem at my beck and call.

I coast up to my garage and dismount, setting foot once more on solid earth—so airy a moment ago. Returning to this plane, I check out my time: a full five minutes longer than my usual "driven" ride—the added cost of dreamtime.

Inclinations

Twenty-three and a half degrees—the angle of inclination of Earth's axis with respect to the ecliptic—that vast plane in space, containing all the planets as they revolve about the Sun. It is the tilt of the spinning Earth that cause its seasons and climate, and the cycles and rhythms of its life. After the fall equinox, the days become shorter than the nights, and we move through wistful fall toward inevitable winter.

My verbena is already aware of the change. It produces no more delicate purple flowers, but it grays and wilts instead. Dead leaves dot the lawn. The impatiens are more optimistic. They still look lush and hardy. But as the weather turns cold, their productivity too will cease, and they will shrink into their earthy resting places. People argue over whether it's the diminishing light or the lowering temperatures that commands the plant world to change. But both are due to those twenty-three and a half degrees of inclination, as Earth sweeps relentlessly along its orbit, tilting now its North Pole, now its South Pole, toward the Sun. Life on Earth, like the planet itself, is acutely tuned to the geometry and phases of the Solar System. The lowly dandelion senses Earth's position better than we humans do—or at least, better than our conscious minds. For in our depths we too must respond to the primal rhythms of the heavens.

We vaguely fathom the majestic pageant of the planets wheeling about the great nurturing Sun, each with its own individual mass, orbital size, tilt angle, periods of revolution and rotation, and family of moons. It all seems perfectly arranged—the giant protective outer planets casting vast gravitational nets to catch rock and ice marauders before they can harm the vulnerable inner planets; Earth, placed between torrid Venus and barren Mars at just the right distance from the Sun for liquid water to form on its surface and provide the matrix for life; and our Moon with its gentle gyrations welling up the oceans into rhythmic tides that breathe oxygenated water into coastal life and cause the waves, currents and winds that enliven the seas and freshen the lands. The marvelous perfection of our Solar System is further accentuated by the recent discoveries of other star-planet systems that are much less favorable to the emergence of life, with their huge Jovian planets careening wildly in eccentric orbits that bring them dangerously close to the central star and forestall any chance for small inner planets, let alone life- nurturing ones. Indeed, a recent book argues that the chances of life existing elsewhere in the universe is diminishingly small—perhaps zero. We may well be alone in the vast cosmos.

But it isn't only the Solar System that is fine tuned to life on Earth. The Sun and its planets were cooked up from the ingredients spewed out in the cataclysmic explosion of a star—a supernova, some five billion years ago. Such events are rare. They occur about once a century in all of the Milky Way Galaxy. And only a supernova can seed space with the essential elements of life—carbon, oxygen, and nitrogen, not to mention the rarer but necessary heavy elements. Such an event must also occur in a large relatively empty region of space. Otherwise, some nearby star could suck up the fresh debris to feed its insatiable gravitational appetite. Thus the structure and evolution of the entire galaxy must be favorable to the birth of a planetary system that can support life. Indeed, the evolution of the entire cosmos must be crucially tuned to allow the existence of just the "right" kind of matter, galaxies, stars and planets, and ultimately, a living Earth.

Not only must Earth be tilted, but the whole universe must be inclined to play the music of the spheres and its rhythms that nurture life and arrange its cycles. The amoeba and the elephant alike, are beholden to such generous and benevolent inclinations. And we humans cannot help but ask who was so inclined?

Eine Kleine Musik
(Excerpt from a memoir, *Music to My Ears*)

I cannot recall a time when I did not love music—when music was not central to my life. Even as a nine-year-old, I was drawn to music as to a seductive siren call.

Walking home from school one day in 1943—P. S. 189 in Manhattan, the very school that the young Maria Callas had attended a dozen years earlier—I tagged along beside Nicholas. I didn't much like Nicholas, but I envied him the violin in its form-fitting alligator case that he carried back and forth to school several times a week. I had often dreamt about taking music lessons and trying to join the school orchestra, but Dad said we couldn't afford a violin.

I grew up in Washington Heights in Manhattan during World War II, just after the Great Depression. My dad was a laborer, working in New York's garment district and, for a spell, selling peanuts and crackerjacks at Madison Square Garden, so we never had much money. Besides, Dad was pretty tight fisted and wouldn't think of throwing his money away on music lessons. It's not that Dad didn't like music. Although baseball was his first love, he had a soft spot for Franz Lehar's *The Merry Widow*, which he had first heard as a teenager in turn-of-the-century Cape Town and then again at the New Amsterdam Theater in New York, shortly after he returned to America in 1908.

Yes, Dad liked music well enough—classical and pop as well as the marvelous operettas and musical shows that exploded on Broadway at the beginning of the 20th century. He just didn't like spending money. He worked too hard to earn the little that he had, so he wasn't about to indulge a kid's whim.

Besides, I'd never shown signs of any real musical talent. I spent hours as a kid sitting at the imposing grand piano that graced my Aunt Ida's living room. But I had to struggle to pick out even the simplest melodies at the keyboard. My musical skills, as I was to discover, were synthetic rather than analytic: I could easily recognize and remember whole melodies and later reproduce them by singing or whistling. But I could not transfer these skills into playing an instrument. I never learned the piano, and although I took up the recorder in later years and could play it reasonably well, it was never natural to me. I could not get past a "first grade" level in my music reading abilities, and sight-reading, which most musicians revel in, was always a horror for me.

And yet listening to music, absorbing it, responding to it deeply, and even becoming obsessed with it were among my greatest joys from early childhood.

Nicholas, my envied violinist acquaintance in fourth grade, played in the school orchestra. Along with a group of other young musicians, all of whom were appointed by heaven in my eyes, he sat high up on that Olympian stage in the school auditorium, and, as if by magic, created beautiful sounds by dragging a bow over the strings that were stretched across his curvy wooden box. I was mystified by how such beauty was produced, but I loved it all the more because of this mystery.

My earliest music recollection is of a rehearsal I witnessed of this revered orchestra. They were working on Mozart's *Eine Kleine Nachtmusik,* a piece written entirely for strings and an ideal choice for our school orchestra, which consisted exclusively of string players. As I listened, I was barely aware of the many interruptions by the conductor, and oblivious to the crude sounds of the undisciplined young musicians. All I heard was an appealing piece—a little longer perhaps than the songs on the radio, but filled with many delights and surprises.

Looking back, I have often wondered what it was in Mozart's miniature gem that managed to hook a nine-year old. Was it the martial fanfare of the opening, the intriguing sequence of the movements, the charming, elegant tunes, the architectural order, or the prevailing zest and spontaneity? Perhaps it had just the right level of structure—neither too simple nor too complex for a young mind. The timing of the experience was serendipitous as well. I was just ripe for it, although I knew nothing about the piece—not its name or composer, nothing about theme and development, movements and tempos, or for that matter, about classical form. All of that would come later. But whatever the mix of fortune and fate, *Eine Kleine Nachtmusik* was a defining moment in my life.

In the weeks that followed, I managed to linger a little at the end of Wednesday school assemblies in the auditorium to catch a few moments of rehearsal—to revel in that infectious "night music." I was haunted by the piece. I whistled and hummed it along with the popular music of the day—*The White Cliffs of Dover, Don't Sit under the Apple Tree with Anyone Else but Me, That Old Black Magic,* and many other World War II ballads and romantic songs of the 1940s. I had begun, in other words, to inhabit a musical world of my own making, an inward realm where I would discover unimagined beauty, meaning and delight.

This inner space contrasted dramatically with my home environment. When I was one and a half, we moved into in a small one-bedroom apartment that my parents had rented "temporarily" while looking for the larger quarters needed for our family. But the Great Depression, World War II, persistent fears about higher rents, and simple resistance to change kept my parents in that apartment for 40 years—until long after I had moved away from home.

In such tight quarters, I did not have my own room nor any real privacy. But fortunately, my parents would often remain after dinner in the kitchen to play cards or entertain neighbors, and I'd have the living room all to myself for a few hours. There, I would read, release my imagination, listen to the radio and play the phonograph. My realm of true solitude and joy was that inner world of music, where I could wander to my heart's delight and discover, like some great explorer, magnificent continents of great depth, scope and beauty.

In that private world, my musical interests developed without benefit of formal training, Although I never acquired much skill in reading music or playing an instrument as a child, my love and appreciation of music continued to blossom through the years and often to preoccupy me as if I were a professional musician. I have even learned to make use of musical scores to deepen my understanding of music. In fact, I own and manage to consult one of the longest and most complex scores ever written—the 823-page complete orchestral score to Wagner's *Die Meistersinger von Nürnberg*. As I listen to recordings of the opera, the score helps me pick out instruments and themes, follow Wagner's complex polyphonies, and understand the architecture of the orchestration. But ask me to play even the simplest line from sheet music on a piano or recorder, and I am as slow and hesitant as a child just beginning to read. Yet neither the lack of scores nor recordings prevented my acquiring a budding "music library." Even before I owned a phonograph, I held in my head a musical repertoire of popular songs and classical works that were constantly enlarged by my radio listening and which I nurtured and treasured like flowers in a musical garden.

Back in fourth grade, I learned to whistle by heart the whole of Mozart's *Eine Kleine Nachtmusik* and I would savor its charms while performing it solo as I walked my dog. When the day arrived for the school concert, I was as nervous and excited as the young musicians. I sat in my seat, hardly able to contain the thrill, following every note of the piece—every theme, every entry—like some junior assistant conductor with an off-stage score, bobbing my head, tapping my fingers and feet, and annoying and puzzling everyone around me. But I hardly cared. It was a triumph for the orchestra—and for me as well. I had attended my first concert and begun my life as a musical connoisseur.

Another favorite of mine at the time was a piano rendition of a showy Latin piece, called *Malagueña*. I would incessantly beg Sybil, an accomplished pianist classmate, to play it for me. She got so sick of it—and of me—that she swore finally never to have anything to do with either of us again. But by then I no longer needed Sybil. I had learned *Malagueña* by heart.

Memory—especially musical memory—is a deep mystery to me. Many tunes and pieces become fixed in the mind and remain there indefinitely. Years later, they can be called up far more readily than names and numbers. Musical memory seems to have its own unique kind of capacity and endurance. I have committed to memory whole symphonies, which in my earlier years I would often "conduct" in the privacy of our living room (although not without occasional peeks by a startled and bewildered parent). Arturo Toscanini, the great 20th-century conductor, was famous for never conducting with a score. But Toscanini was no marvel to me. I never used a score to conduct either.

Listening to the radio one night, I heard a piece that sounded like something played by the Pied Piper himself. It thoroughly bewitched me. I strained to hear the title, but all I could catch was something like "Ravelspaleri." I hung on to that snatch of a title and inquired about it for days, but no one seemed to know what I was talking about. After a few weeks, I had almost completely forgotten about it. Then, one Saturday morning, Mom took me downtown to Radio City Music Hall. In the 1940s, the Music Hall was already famous for mounting lavish stage shows to accompany the movies. After several exciting scenes, there was a big production number by the Rockettes, who danced with Busby Berkely precision. I thought that must be the grand finale. But then, the stage and the theater darkened and the orchestra was mysteriously elevated from its pit.

My mother whispered to me that the conductor was Alexander Smallens, whom she had actually known as a child. Smallens waited for complete silence, and then signaled the snare drum to begin its hypnotic rat-a-tat-tat rhythm, soon to be joined by a lone flute exhaling into the darkened auditorium the sinuous fumes of its haunting theme. I lurched forward in my seat, recognizing this as that very "spaleri" piece I had given up on. But Radio City, Alexander Smallens and the orchestra were not merely about to jog my memory. This was the real finale, a truly spectacular one. As the music began to open up and swell, the dark stage slowly brightened to reveal dancers in tropical costumes, swaying and leaping to the ravishing melody. More performers slipped on to the stage, increasing the gyrating throng, as one by one the instruments of the orchestra joined the ranks of sound and imperceptibly quickened the pace.

As the serpentine melody grew and filled our ears, an army of drummers in golden loincloths and breastplates appeared on small balconies all around the huge auditorium to reinforce the swelling sound. Now, the orchestra at full volume released the tension with a climactic shift to E-major, while the stage erupted in voluptuous dancing and pageantry, and the surrounding drums thundered the relentless rhythm. The colossal orgy ended abruptly with a final explosive chord, followed by an awestruck silence; then oceans of applause.

I had discovered Maurice Ravel's *Bolero*.

Forgery

No more ink,
nothing wet.
Just fine black powder
sprayed on paper and bonded in a flash
of electrostatic forgery.
Letters, words, sentences appear
faster than meteors
fizzing and sputtering through the atmosphere.
Quills, lead, even rolling balls—
things of the past.
Poems and stories conjured today
by Maxwell's demons and Schrödinger's cats.

Imagine *Hamlet* emerging
on a Hewlett-Packard laser jet.
Never mind a million monkeys
typing for a million years.
Now it's countless motes of black dust
shooting through space,
falling willy-nilly on the white surface,
cast into shapes and forms
that say, "To be or not to be."
Well is it?
Is dust destined to speak,
to replace ink and even thought?

Vernelle Kurak

Vernelle Erickson Kurak comes from a long line of card players and storytellers. Since neither of these avocations proved to be cost-effective, Vernelle fell back upon disparate and more mundane occupations such as number crunching, academic edification, matrimony and motherhood. She has been a member of the 42nd Street Irregulars for ten years

Ruthie and Company

"There, let's eat there," I exclaimed. My unerring gourmand eye had spotted the restaurant sign two blocks away even though the early evening was dusky with rain.

"Maybe we should drive around some more," my husband ventured.

"No, I'm tired. It's hot and muggy. We've been on the road all day. The U.P. is pretty monotonous in a pouring rain. Plus I'm hungry."

"You know how you are, Sweetheart. Nothing but the best is good enough for you! There might be just the place to suit you...." My husband's voice dwindled off as I speeded the car up a bit.

"That's one advantage to doing all the driving," I thought. "We stop where I want to stop." I peered ahead through the mist. Now I could make out the lighted restaurant sign. "The House of Ludington," I said. "At least they're trying to be a little up-scale. Plus, it's right on the lakeshore."

"I don't care where it is as long as the food's good," my husband grumbled, conceding reluctantly.

Soon we were inside the restaurant and quickly seated by the hostess in a corner of the semi-dark dining room. I looked around the room. It was decorated in upper-Midwestern old English, the dark oak paneling sopping up the weak wattage from the ornate chandeliers.

"I wish we could have had a table by the window," I said. "Look, there's plenty of room there. We could look out at Lake Michigan."

"Let's just order something, Dear. It's going to be dark soon anyway. Miss!" He hailed a passing waitress, "Please, Miss. I need a beer. Do you have anything on tap?"

Reluctantly, I focused my attention on the menu as the waitress started her litany of available beers.

"Nothing on tap, sir," she said, "but in the bottle we have Grain Belt, Grain Belt Lite, Summit, Summit Pale Ale, Heinekens..."

"I'll have a bottle of Heinekens." My husband's choice was no surprise to me; he always ordered Heinekens.

The waitress turned to leave. "You would think she could have asked me if I wanted anything," I thought.

"Miss, just a minute." I spoke to her departing back while noting that her green uniform blouse was torn at the left armhole.

When she stopped and turned back toward me I said, "I was wondering if you had any specials today?"

"I'm not your waitress. Emily Ann is. I'll send her over in a minute," she said as she once again turned and hurried toward the bar.

In due course Emily Ann arrived, as did my husband's beer. The special, she told us, was roast turkey with mashed potatoes and corn-on-the-cob.

"I'll have that," my husband said eagerly. Corn-on-the-cob is a favorite of his. He would never notice that it had been standing around in hot water for an hour.

"Tell me," I said, "do you make the mashed potatoes from real potatoes or from those dried flakes?"

"Oh, we make them from real potatoes. Potatoes grown right here on the U.P." Emily Ann's reply encouraged me to order the special, too. I could always trade my corn-on-cob for my husband's mashed potatoes.

Emily Ann brought us a big basket of hard rolls. They were warm, too. I took one, buttered it and took a big bite. "Mmmm, good," I said. "Maybe the food will live up to the restaurant's name rather than to its decor." I felt better already.

I idly scanned the room as I waited for the "special" to arrive. It is one of my hobbies to "people-watch" to see if I can figure out their stories. My husband calls it "eavesdropping," but I notice he is eager enough to hear my speculations.

As I buttered another roll, I noticed a threesome entering the dining room. There were two older women, perhaps in their sixties, and one young woman maybe in her twenties.

"Let's watch and see if they get a table by the window," I said, already formulating my complaint about our table if they were. "No, the hostess is bringing them over toward our little backwater."

I looked at the three as they trailed the hostess somewhat haphazardly through the tables and across the room. The two older women were obviously dressed up for a special occasion. The heavier one wore a rose pastel cotton suit with a white-bowed blouse. A white poplin hat decorated with pink and green foliage casually perched on her blue-gray hair.

The other older woman, buxom but trim, was perfectly groomed in a navy-blue suit over a ruby-red blouse. A matching navy-blue hat, accented with a red ribbon, sat squarely on the top of her artificially auburn hair.

The young woman was casual in blue jeans and a tee shirt that read, "Ya ain't seen nothin' yet..." Now that I had a better look at the young woman, I saw that she was blonde and eighteen or nineteen at the most.

I speculated to myself that the young woman might even be that rarity of nature, a natural blonde. "I'm going to call the three of them 'White Hat', 'Blue Hat' and *The Blonde* .'Let the play begin.'" I thought as I laughed aloud at my bon mot. I took another hard roll.

I noted that Blue Hat clung uncertainly to White Hat's left arm even though The Blonde held firmly onto Blue Hat's right arm. In this erratic fashion the three finally made it to the table adjacent to ours.

The Blonde spoke to Blue Hat. "Here now. This is the chair. If you move to your left a bit and around it, we can get you seated."

Blue Hat obeyed. As she sank with obvious relief into the chair she announced loudly, "It isn't easy to be blind, you know."

The hostess passed out menus to the three women. "Your server today will be Emily Ann. Enjoy your dinners." After she spoke her piece the hostess hurried back to the reception desk where more customers waited.

White Hat and Blue Hat launched into the preliminaries.

Blue Hat: "I'm going to have spring lamb."

White Hat: "They don't have any spring lamb listed. I see turkey is today's special. Maybe I'll have the turkey." She sounded undecided.

Blue Hat: "Turkey! Turkey! I can have that anytime. I have to have something I can eat. No lamb, you say? Do they have lake trout?"

The two of them sputtered on about their orders. I grew tired of my little eavesdropping drama. Also, the rolls were all gone. I began to despair for our order. I looked around for our waitress. Surely our dinners were ready by now. They undoubtedly sat cooling on the service counter waiting for Emily Ann.

What parent would name their child Emily Ann anyway? What was this, the nineteenth century? Just at that moment Emily Ann reappeared, but not with our dinners. Order pad in hand, she went instead to the threesome's table. "Would you like something to drink before you order?" she said smiling.

The Blonde said, "I'll have a Coke. Classic, please—and a glass."

"Do you have spring lamb?" demanded Blue Hat.

"No, I'm sorry we don't, but we do have turkey," Emily Ann replied, still smiling. "Could I bring you a cocktail?"

"No lamb? I was counting on it. You used to have such good lamb here." Blue Hat's voice boomed out emphatically.

White Hat spoke up, "Why don't we have a drink before we order?" She turned toward the waitress. " I'll have Scotch on the rocks. Cutty Sark on the rocks with water on the side."

"Yes, Cutty Sark on the rocks for me, too. A double. And make sure it's Cutty Sark. I can't drink that bar scotch," Blue Hat said. "And you might as well take our orders now, too. I will have the turkey after all. Turkey's supposed to be good for you, no fat."

White Hat agreed on turkey for her dinner as well. The Blonde's order was as inaudible as the older women's was raucous.

"Miss! Miss! Emily Ann!" I called out to our waitress as she hurried past. "What about our orders? We have been waiting for a long time."

"Don't worry, they're coming." Emily Ann said, barely glancing toward us as she hurried back toward the kitchen.

When the threesome's drinks arrived (very quickly, I noted), the Blue Hat raised her glass in a toast, "To our protégée!"

"Yes, to Lee Ann," White Hat said.

Click, click, click went their glasses. They drank deeply.

"Don't you want another beer?" I said to my husband.

"Not much chance of getting another even if I wanted one. Our waitress is busy with that table next to us." He said as he smiled and nodded toward our neighbors.

"What's that man smiling about? You, sir, what are you smiling about?" Blue Hat, the supposedly blind woman fixed my husband with a cold and accusing stare.

I suppressed the urge to laugh as my husband, always adroit at extricating himself from situations he has bumbled into, explained his smile by saying, "I couldn't help but observe your sophisticated preservation of the ritual of toasting. I am delighted to see that it is an art not entirely extinct."

For White Hat and Blue Hat his response was as good as a formal introduction. They proceeded to tell us of their long trip from home to bring the young blonde, Lee Ann, to start her first year in a nursing program at De Noc College.

"She's our protégée. We've been taking care of her for years. Now we're here to see her settled in for her first year of college. We're so proud," said White Hat. Blue Hat gushed her agreement. The Blonde, now known as Lee Ann and all the less interesting for it, looked bored. I tried to peek around discreetly in hopes of spying our errant dinners. Emily Ann brought another round for everyone including water for me.

The topic turned to my husband's occupation. "You teach school?" Lee Ann asked, suddenly alert. My husband admitted as much.

"You teach English? Oh, we need that. We need to get rid of all those 'dis', 'dat' and 'dose'. I get so tired of hearing that. " Blue Hat gestured grandly for emphasis as she spoke; then she finished her second double shot, neat.

"You know, Ruthie here," White Hat said as she indicated Blue Hat. "Ruthie here majored in English."

"That's right I did. And if you ever want to know about one of dose—those—split participles, don't ask these young ones here." Blue Hat a.k.a. Ruthie glared meaningfully at Lee Ann as she spoke.

Thankfully, Emily Ann bringing the salads to our table halted our budding acquaintance. Ruthie and company fell back into conversation amongst themselves. I concentrated on my salad glad to be freed from the eccentricities of our neighbors at the next table.

Emily Ann, the waitress, who had served us salads of quite ordinary iceberg lettuce dressed in a mediocre blue cheese dressing, soon brought the trio, Ruthie and company as I now thought of them, three elaborate concoctions. Huge mounds of multi-colored, cool fruits topped with swirly towers of whipped cream, pebbled over with ripe, red cherries all of which rested on a green fan of exotic lettuce leaves. I watched with envious craving.

Ruthie started to pop cherry after cream-laden cherry into her mouth, talking all the while. I imagined that I could see the whipped cream and cherry juice dribble down her chin.

I turned back to my own poor salad, taking care to set aside the rusty bits of lettuce. After a bite or two I stole a quick look at Ruthie's salad. She wasn't eating it anymore.

Ruthie, who had until now re-centered her blue hat firmly on her head every few minutes suddenly seemed subdued. One of her hands clutched a napkin that she held to her lips again and again in an almost spastic motion. Her blue hat with its red ribbon was definitely askew.

There was something wrong. I tried not to look at her. She was going to be sick, right here in front of me. And I wouldn't be able to eat my dinner. In spite of myself, I kept glancing over at her. My distress grew with Ruthie's. Why don't they leave? "Please leave!" I begged silently. My delight at their eccentricities was dissipated by revulsion. At last, Ruthie's apparent affliction caught the attention of her companions.

"Ruthie's sick," White Hat stated.

"No, she's all right. Just drink some water, Mrs. Bransford. You'll be O.K." Lee Ann's formal address of her mentor surprised me even as I noted that the young blonde barely halted her fork in mid-bite to deliver her opinion.

"No. Ruthie's sick. She's having a heart attack. Get the waitress over here. Miss! Over here, please. Miss, I want you to cancel our dinners. Ruthie here is having a heart attack; we've got to get her outside," White Hat said firmly. "Yes, that's right. Cancel our dinners -- that was three turkeys. Can you do that?" White Hat, like Lee Ann, seemed matter of fact in her assessment. But at least she was acting. She got up and went around to Ruthie's chair. She patted Ruthie on the shoulder and shouted in her ear, "Come on, Ruthie. We'll have to take you outside. I've cancelled our dinners."

"Just get her to drink water. She'll be O.K. Here." As she spoke, Lee Ann grabbed a huge water glass and held it to Ruthie's mouth. "Just take a big drink. Then swallow. You'll be all right," she said.

White Hat joined Lee Ann in the emergency treatment. They tilted Ruthie's head back to force the water down her throat. Ruthie's hands flailed in the air and she dropped her napkin. The water poured down Ruthie's chin; Lee Ann mopped at it with her own napkin.

The waitress, Emily Ann, who like me had watched in frozen fascination, finally moved. "I'll get the doctor," she said. "He lives upstairs. He's a bachelor." Her hands went to her hair and she fluffed it out. She licked her lips and straightened her uniform skirt; then she hurried off through the kitchen door where several of the other restaurant staff had already fled. After what seemed an eternity, the waitress was back.

"The doctor'll be here soon. He's getting dressed," she said flushing slightly. She again turned and almost ran back into the inner reaches of the kitchen. I sat immobile, willing the doctor to come before it was too late. Could it be that this woman would die at the table next to us? Could it be that those three who were such characters would ultimately ruin my dinner? No, surely not. Not at the next table.

The doctor walked briskly through the kitchen doorway.

"You look quite blue," the doctor said to Ruthie. Even as he was diagnosing her color the doctor was pulling her from her chair. He reached around her middle from behind and gave her a sharp squeeze." There. It's out now. It was something stuck in your throat. A cherry!" he said and held up the offending cherry for all to see." Didn't anyone here think of squeezing her," he scolded.

Everyone, all of us who had not squeezed Ruthie, relaxed. Our turkey dinners finally came. They were really quite good except that the corn-on-the-cob was watery. Even my husband thought so. One should never order corn-on-the-cob in a restaurant. Ruthie and company still sat next to us, White Hat having instructed the waitress to bring them three turkey dinners after all.

Now it was Lee Ann, the young protégée, who was voluble. "Have you ever noticed how hard it is for people to die?" she said. "Being born is easy, but it's hard to die. You really have to work at it." Lee Ann polished off the rest of her salad and then, eyeing the still splendid remainder of Ruthie's salad with noticeable regret, she lit a cigarette. "You know, after we leave here, let's stop at the disco. Just to have a drink and see what's going on," she said cheerfully.

White Hat brightened. "Yes," she said. "We could stop at the disco. Just to have a drink and see what it's like. Maybe they have a live band."

Ruthie didn't say anything, and when I looked at her, I noticed that her hat had slipped just a bit more to one side.

The Birch Root

Tired from the rising path above the roiling Brule
I took my rest upon the birch root
There where it stretched across the foot-worn path.
Wide-kneed like an ambivalent tree toad
Seeking warmth from the pale sun,
I sat.

I studied then the root, my temporary roost.
It crawled twelve feet across the gravel-gray surface
Seeking secure anchor, a chink in the bed rock
To hold its tree back from the precipice,
Where it yearned toward the swirling waters
Far below.

I listened too, heard the rush and gurgle of the Brule, busy
Rounding stones and scouring out red kettles.
A breeze flicked through the yellowed leaves; I shivered,
Chilled with hint of frost.
Huddled there, I took strength from the undaunted root,
Wished for a breath of hot balsam from summer past.

 I arose then to go on upward toward the falls;
My departing feet scuffed tiny pebbles,
Making small note of my passing.
Does my body's warmth still linger where I sat upon
        the root?
In the winter snow, will it sometimes feel my weight?

Or was I like summer ephemera?
Who are born, who dance, who die,
While the birch root holds its mother tree
And the Brule scours out red kettles.

That Tree....

As December closed the aging year,
I saw you there.
You stood silent on the narrow boulevard.

I pondered sadly on your muteness.
Did you grieve for branches sawed by
Cruel November surgeons --
Who careless
Hacked your lower limbs--
Fed them to the chipper,
There in the aura of your pain?
Did you endure bereft the arctic night,
An amputee, feeling lost limbs sway in the wind?
See their shadows moon-cast upon the snow,
Perhaps imagine lizard feet of clinging birds?

April brought you amber tears, damp on each wound.
I wept with you then, regretting all.

Now sootheful May brings new-budded leaves
Fashions you a crown of yellow green.
The red Cardinal, an eager lover,
Perches among your upper branches
To trill a love song to his mate.

He prompts me to your side;
I touch your trunk in wonder.
There round the scars of last year's sorrow

I see small branches sprout anew.

Bluff Country Windmill
In Memory of My Brother

On the bleak limestone bluff
The whirling wheel of the
Old abandoned windmill creaks and groans.
Balanced on a steel-legged tower,
The windmill's daisy wheel of metal blades
Is still obedient to its trailing vane.
First, the vane stands straight behind, then cants.
The wheel slows, shows its gap-toothed age,
Turns to face the stiff March gale,
Spins again,
Newly impelled.

A ring of blue-black
Junipers crowns the rounded bluff.
There the windmill stands,
Where, in the past, a farm and farmer were.
The back slope of the bluff
Is dotted with tufts of grass once grazed by cattle,
Stock that climbed the hill
To drink deep from the watering tank filled
By the working windmill.

The grass clumps,
Brown polka-dots against the thin white snow,
Now feed tiny scurrying birds that
Race zigzag from tuft to tuft,

Suffering the scouring blast.
At the base of the hill, two highways meet;
Snarling traffic slows, stops for the crossing,
Roars on again.

High above it all
The muttering traffic,
The small birds gathering grass seeds,
The dark, silent junipers,
The whirling wheel of the solitary windmill
Alone in the timeless sky,
A hawk circles, riding the updraft,
Coasting the cruel wind.

Joyce Mellstrom

Joyce Mellstrom has been churning out words in rhythm, rhyme and helter skelter ever since (just out of the cradle) she discovered people would listen, laugh, cry, give her candy, and excuse her from phy. ed. The rewards just keep getting subtler and more precious. So does the poetry.

Hand-Made

There were four of us going from diapers to elementary
    school.
The diapers, as you know, were interchangeable.
Why not the mittens as well? thought my enterprising
    and overwhelmed mother.
So she knit,
As in the fairy tale where swans became brothers as jackets
    reeled off the heroine's needles,
Exemplary mittens of green and white stripe.
Flip the left over flapjack style and it became the right.
Lose one and another and another took its place.
An excellent way to beat the odds when
Four little girls leave mittens on the playground,
In the gutter, on a bench in the cloakroom or in any of
    the secret spots that
All the world's children discover to deposit their treasures
    and castoffs.
Then one wintry, gusty day, the stash of mittens that
    doled out daily
The covering for eight hands
Would come up short
(How many times this happened is beyond the scope
    of our speculation.)

Then the mother dressed up and walked,
As her children did in the days before school buses
    and pedophiles,

113

To the brick building with the varnished floors and women
        teachers and only
one or two thugs
(This was the fifties. We yearn for them. They've vanished
        beyond a distant flagpole.)
Mrs. Mellstrom in heels, negotiating snowdrifts or puddles
        with icing, to secure
a batch of mittens
For the next onslaught of winter.
The box that held all orphan head and hand gear
Held out by the office secretary to one child after another
        and the occasional
optimistic mother,
Gave forth with its mildewed odor (for these items are
        often lost during
snowball fights and snow angel construction), an odd
        number of green
and white striped hand shapes belonging to four girls
        who were only
beginning to realize the value of things like mittens
        and moms.
Mrs. Mellstrom strode home then with her bounty and
        made a second pot of coffee.
No neighbors drifted by, as in summer.
The clock ticked and maybe she knit another pair, just to be
On the safe side, the fifties side, the side where civil defense
        made sense and
Four girls' lost mittens returned like homing pigeons.

Violet Morning

One o-so-early a.m., I rode a bicycle
Straight up into the cloudless air,
Looking for your well-sequestered
Bed chamber.
And when I got there,
The sheets were not but soon would be
In shocking disarray.
Our pants on fire felt like hearts.
We shredded propriety,
Threw caution to one side,
Balanced on a mattress as angels do on a pin,
Traded real estate from mouth to mouth
Fired off cannons from each nerve.
Time was limited:
This was a morning affair, after all.
Your boss and mine
Had one gimlet eye for the clock,
Another for us.
So we tap tap tapped that 9 to 5 dance,
Me counting sleep, you the boss's advances.
Not soon enough, it was 5 a.m. again.
The hill leading to your bed, then sheer cliff and a great fall.
We can laugh about it now:
Divorces final, addresses combined,
Ex-spouses so ex they neither stalk nor seethe.
Times like this—
Lovers' spat or misjudged moment that swells

To Beethoven's Ninth complete with chorus—
I might do worse than recall
How high I pedaled
How hard huffed and puffed
To blow your house down.
And what singular notes you sang
When we nestled just now for the millionth time.

DAD as He Lies Dying

They give haircuts like I cut grass, these folks from Jamaica
and the world over,
but not from here. No Swedes to take care of Swedes or
Germans to take crap from demented old Germans.
And so, his tufts of hair resemble clumps of mismatched
blades:
His gray, theirs green in a lawn neglected—that word fits
too, here in this nursing home.
Case in point:
His clothes walk away, says my sis, and I picture them
clumping down the hall
As I do—intent on leaving a place soaked in urine and
regret, leavings of humans
Dumped in soiled beds or deposited momentarily before
plates of pale meat.
I'm not yet content to let him lie in the shade of his
silent mind, still think
There are spots of sunlight to be investigated for their
unknown import.
Could be he'll bring up our almost trip to Alaska (delayed,
at the last moment, for fifty years) or the nice house
the family never bought but might have.
The bleakness of his mind no longer holds those shades
of the dead that populated his yard the first year he slid
out of reality.
Now they've gone off to be angels or push up tulips
or spoil under six feet of forgetfulness.

Now they've left him to his own or no devices, a happier
    camper for that,
Given the tears that watered each remembrance those last
    months of *compos mentis*.
Failing to resolve any of my doubts and out of the
    ever-smaller talk ,
Talk that falls barren on his
Exhausted soil, I give him a chocolate to melt in his toothless
    mouth, wondering briefly where his dentures have
    gone (perhaps with the clothes, they've walked)
Dutiful daughter for the moment, I massage his stiff hands
    to produce the smile that can let me leave without
    ensuing nightmares:
Then I too can walk away.

'58 Fairlane

Ford Fairlane, new as a baby's tooth:
The family troops out dutifully to admire.
"It's a surprise!" my dad says
To 1, 2, 3, 4 girls positioned in size
Leading up to Mom, whose face stays a mask.
It's no shock to her, since he brings home new cars
Oftener than I bring home stray cats;
Oftener than the gas man suggests,
If you don't pay now, it's curtains for the heat.

The looking done, the crowd disperses—
I to *Ribsy & Beezus*, little kids to dolls and dirt,
Mom to her sewing machine,
Where she cranks out four of everything
From a remnant the size of Montana.
"Matching!" she cajoles when our faces betray
A knowledge that fashion is not served by her needle.

"God damn it to hell!" she explodes to her Singer,
When we're tucked into bed and the Fairlane
Has taken Dad to the bar where his dreams
And our nightmares take shape.

From the room we four share I hear her curse,
Then watch round-eyed till his return,
Watch the shadow angel hover on the ceiling
Where the closet door's been left ajar.
Take in the muffled exchange when he's parked his machine

And hers has issued four spring wardrobes of blue plaid.
A lamp finds the floor, an eye darkens in the discussion
that ensues.

Off Leash

Just now a Samoyed-sized wave broadsided my dog.
She was standing kattywampus to the lake, confident of
    the maximum the shore could rearrange itself.
Then: Whoop de doo! That tenth wave had the strength of
    the first nine!
And she was capsized—nearly—by the punk.
Her startled look said "What the hey?
Can't a dog be sure of anything now'days?"
She'd been a trooper all the live-long day:
Launching her careful self across a stream that smacked of
WATERFALLS AHEAD!
Endured my raspberry picking far too long,
On a sun-drenched dirt road, she hotly encased in fur.
Suffered the indignity of being hefted
(all 80 pounds) up a daunting boulder,
Followed by further humiliation as I backed
Her bulk down a tiny cliff
(The way led past: It wasn't my fault.)
Then, later, it *was* my fault:
I got us hopelessly lost on the hottest and dustiest trail.
No primo views in sight, as I peered into the brushy depths
To find our tent, so small—and gray as the gloom
    of November,
Though it was sunny August where we wandered.
I said, "I'll make it up to you." I tried.
But all she gets is grief—now from the mighty lake
Back then from me,
Whose claim to be your guardian's been vastly strained

By one after another unwise predicament on this, our
        maiden voyage
Into camping together. But admit,
You dirty and now wet but not forsaken pooch:
It's worth all pain to lay your sodden fur
On these storm-smoothed Superior rocks,
Look in vain for the opposite shore as your brown
        eyes travel
Over cliff line, island peninsula, and most of all:
Those safely-navigated, now more distant waves,
The mad sloshing of a lake tired of soothing tourists,
And thinking of claiming a body, human or not.

You needed to be upset, smug city pooch, and so did I.
The fangs this lake shows give me (and you) pause.
Whet my appetite for something in a storm,
A wave gigantic enough to bark about—
Or write a poem if it comes to that,
Then, melancholy, beat, retire to our tent to hear the roar.
Dreaming, you'll curl your lip and growl at the
        shoreline's threat,
Waking, I'll hear a strenuous way to live,
When we're back in the city, each on her own leash.

What the Customer Never Saw

Fast forward through a chaotic Saturday night to 1:20 a.m.
A sofa-sized sink invites you to scrub cushion-size pans
Summon the elbow grease to scour baked potato from
    600 steak dinners
Before morning light irradiates the kitchen's gloom
And the time clock awaits your next punch.

Back the tape up to 10 p.m., shank of evening & customer
    & cow.
An ashtray holds the waitress' focus as she looks for
    her shade of lipstick among six.
She inhales an iron lung-full of Pall Mall straight
On the run
Then it's through the swinging door with her to their world:
Martinis, manhattans, clinking glasses
Meek wives who pocket the tip beneath the plate
As Ansel glares, not meek but silent
That tip was her babies' next meal or her own next
    whiskey bottle.

At times like this, the bustle threatens confusion in the
    ashtray—
Though never in the chef's array of orders—
Did she really light *two* Pall Malls?
Or has Madge, Katie, Dot switched brands?
In which case, what subtle lipstick shade is yours?
Carmen or flame?

Faster, faster their fannies heave the swinging door

To night mavens' haunt

Set down the giant platters that hold every delicacy from
tenderloin to T-bone.

Black poly uniforms hide the sweat

White nurse's shoes maintain the fevered pace.

Quarters, dimes, dollars make their way into and leave
her pocket

Before settling up and down time.

She doles out to busboy and hostess, counts her own

Pronounces it meager in view of the bunions

Leaves her daughters scrubbing the tinfoil potato blankets
off sheets of metal

To their particular woes.

We scrub, long into the night, while her quarters form neat
piles on the dresser

And her hose, uniform, bunions soak out the day.

In Couples Therapy

She #1:Your love is like a washing machine, so many cycles,
from delicate and hand wash
To sturdy, heavy duty, crushing the dirt of my thoughts to
smithereens,
So sudsy, I break down under your assault

She #2:My love, you spend way too much money.

She #1:Do that shouting thing like you're a police siren and
I'm asphalt.

She #2: Can I borrow your blue dress?

She #1:You need new clothes. I can't touch my own clothes
on you!
I'm Paul Bunyan. You're Babe the Blue Ox. We travel
together across Minnesota, making lakes wherever we
go. Licking deviled eggs off my fingers today, you took
my foolish heart again by storm.
In a room that smelled of old passions gone moldy, we
lounged so late the concierge of the hotel called to
scatter us so the room could be made up. Housekeep-
ing waits for lovers only so long, even in France. In
Paris, you get more leeway to be a slut, stay out all
night festering with decadence, maybe have your first
French trick and not know his name in the morning.

What do you do with your tongue to make it find those
	parts so far inside I'd forgotten if I ever knew that
	they existed?
What arousal plans do you have to put on the dress so tight
	that my eyes can trace your geography hill and dale.
When I sat next to you today and listened to your recital of
	past resentment, anger, and fear, I leapt to my feet and
	admonished you to stop. I held my judgment long
	enough to let that hair I love and that springs so
	strongly under my hand—I'm pimping again I know
	but I can't help this letter across enemy lines and that
	has to pass censors so I can't say entirely what's on my
	mind but resort to innuendo, matchless beauty, so
	strange to have you in my clutches and how long has it
	been?

Sweater Weather

Those with physiques to show
Are skipping this season to peel off in a rush
Long sleeves, foot coverings, hats, belts, pants with cuffs,
To unbury shortest shorts—
(Flaunting plumage more dire than mere comfort to these
young.)

Settled in middle age and taking my body there with me,
I must gather courage to expose such dubious contours as
Flapping arm skin, thunder thighs.
So it's sweater weather for me:
A lusciously cool chance to stride down avenues arced with
tree giants
Disproportionately leafed with tiny bits of green.
My sweater forgives the gracelessness of 55 years.
My bouncing step mirrors those of steppers with only
20 springs
To recall and hold dear.
Renewal pays no heed to an oak's age or mine,
Paints a vision of June busting out and me forgetting
Winter's troubling murk.
Swinging cloaked arms, I attempt a cartwheel
To astound the five-year old at my side.
"You're too old," she exclaims,
after executing the proper leg-high pinwheel version
with ease.

My heart disagrees
But having made peace with so many of my own frowns,
Hers merely echoes down the stream of years ahead as a
challenge:
Take the burnished memories of cartwheel days into all the
sweater weather to come.

Widower's Blues

The bottle's by your side. You drink. You stare.
A phone rings loudly as the last sip's poured.
The dog sleeps fretful at your feet, or bored.
You pass some hours in the TV's glare.

She swore before her death: "This man is mine.
His brown eyes, sweet intentions, and the gift
For coming home with flowers after a rift."
Then "We loved too much and had to pay the fine,"

Said that waitress, working late so you could coo,
Take refuge in the arms of Marge or June or Viv.
Enough that your kiss got her where she lived.
Love, like the stuff you guzzle's a strange brew.

Leaves a poor man howling at the moon.
Leaves a woman in her grave too soon.

Diane Pecoraro

Diane Pecoraro has been writing since the age of twelve when she found a thick blank-lined notebook on the beach in Rye, New York. Then, she used to read her words out loud to anyone who would listen. Nowadays, she tends to stash her finished and unfinished poems back into notebooks—still lined, which sit on the left side of her desk. Once or twice, she has ventured out and submitted her work. On one of those occasions, she won second prize in an AAUW poetry contest. Bureaucrat by day, writer of verse during the dark hours, she mines all 24 hours as material for her serious and not-so-serious poems.

The Year 2002: At Sixty

It's her shoulder, his knee,
Another's arteries to the heart,
High blood pressure here, cholesterol there,
We're collectively falling apart.

It's her hemorrhoids, his prostate,
The occasional renegade fart,
Aching joints joined to aching limbs,
Collectively we're falling apart.

The bad back so often lamented,
Surgical scar now a fine chest dart,
Memory leaks at a more frequent drip,
When did it start—this falling apart?

He got a hearing aid sometime in May
From the super prosthesis mart,
Injections of insulin daily dosed,
Have I said that we're falling apart?

Alterations in the once reliable bod,
Fountain of youth's now the geyser of geezer,
It seems to help to talk this out,
Collective kvetching* at least makes it easier.

*Kvetching—from the Yiddish, to complain

Elegy for Indigo*

If people could be animals, she would be a cat,
A grand tabby pulled up and imposing,
A ginger presence first above, then below eye level,
In a leap looking down at you, next sidling low.
A cat who spends winter afternoons asleep alone
Centered on a quilt in the small sunny bedroom,
Or catching up on conversation, fur brushing ankles,
Slyly companionable—but for one minute only.

If people could be animals, she would be a cat,
A grand Abyssinian regal and gold-eyed,
Although lineage and breed are never an issue
Given all the strays she's counted around multiple bowls
Set at stop points in kitchen and bath. Like the kitten
Plucked from a drain pipe, or the frightened gray
Shivering in a Pamida parking lot in late January's chill.
She wrapped him in her designer coat, loaded him in
    the back seat,
And made him one of her larger family of cats and people,
Wide-ranging clutter and exuberant bouquets.

*Indigo was Elizabeth's beloved cat who died. This was written
during the grieving process (2000).

Seeing Stories: Truchas, New Mexico
For Vincent

It tells a story, you say,
Standing before this bramble-filled grave,
An accidental stop along the High Road to Taos,
The dry sacred ground of a Mexican cemetery
Circled by one far peak blending into another,
A vast ring of low-volt violet haze in late afternoon.

Objects, each perfectly placed,
Honor the dead and remind the living.
What holds us? The pair of black sunglasses
Mounted on the rusted motorcycle frame,
Or the folded letters signed with girl names that coo
Of love? A life snuffed at twenty–three, it unsettles,
Leaves strands unresolved, asking, irresistibly asking,
To be tied together.

A day later you recite your dream,
A story of emotional element,
Narrative seeps from the pebbles
Of deep canyons, phantom turns visible
Only during night's tossing, dramas
Of spirit and place on a mind stage,
A thousand and one nights, a thousand stories,
Stoked by day flickers in red.

From fragments of smoke and line
A new tale is forged, rises mysteriously

From mounds heaped with spirit offerings.
The buried shards of memory, ours, theirs
Form a unique melody that sings
Completely of the self.

Exhibit of Roy DeCarava's Photos
Two Couples Dancing, Group at Table

Truth is, you know, on some nights
they could torch the walls with their anger,
beer-ignited, hardship fueled,
recurrent couple cankers exposed to neighbors
climbing the stairs with their own bundles
but stopping anyway to hear insults and betrayals
hurled like marbles down a long tenement hall.
Fury lavished on each other when
there is nowhere else to put it.

That may be the truth—one part of it. The other
caught here, the soft-rubbed edge of Saturday night,
a sashay away from a week's hard work,
two couples dancing in a cramped kitchen,
chrome and linoleum turned jazz club.
Whatever music is playing on the radio
(maybe it's Billie* moved from another portrait),
whatever unfiltered smoke fills the air,
they're pressed together and you can feel the heat,
not heat so much as warmth, the comfort
of body pressed against familiar body swaying
in fine rhythm, knees grazing, torsos touching,
a temporary night song to cast bluesy shadows
off the chipped enamel of an old Frigidaire.

*Billie Holiday, singer

Postcard from Vernelle
Le Bon Genre: Les Trois Graces

Buried between the bill from Bloomingdales,
The handyman flyer to fix it—all of it,
The estate protection course calendar,
Tax bill, electric bill, car statement,
Survey from public television,
Promise of senior supplements,
A New Yorker demanding to be read,
Sweepstakes with possible lucky number,
The discreet letter to singles,
Premature pre-holiday catalogues,
And the message from His Holiness, The Dalai Lama,
Is the postcard from Vernelle.

Three delicately drawn buxom charmers,
Les Trois Graces du Ballet,
Arms entwined in a dance of maidens,
Models of the latest cinched waists balanced
By extravagant head coverings suggesting Greece
With a nod to the Orient,
Their toes pointed in oblique positions,
A puff of early 1800's French flair.

On the back, Vernelle writes
"Six days in Paris is not enough"
And I know that, by now, she has performed at least
One grand arabesque on one of the grand boulevards,
Forgetting in that echoing moment
Her sore and aching feet.

Sausage

Suddenly it's about sausage,
A stew that she has made for Christmas eve,
Polish set in sauerkraut spiked with caraway,
and as she speaks, the ooze of vinegar and the heft
    of kielbasa
are in my mouth filling my mind and her memory
with times when sausage was not an outlaw food
but the filling, often with cheese, of sandwiches
unwrapped daily in the school cafeteria
to be traded with chums if their choice of the day
happened to be tastier than yours.

No matter that we grew up on different continents,
we both knew those special shops,
wonderlands where stalactites of dried salami, all sizes,
hung from the ceiling and behind the glass case,
the moist, more pampered, Swedish, Italian, Hungarian,
and a man, always a man, offering a sample
sliced very thin, handed over the counter
on a piece of wax paper, a spicy wafer to savor,
the reward of a forced morning trek to the local market.

Sausage as celebration, consolation, barter.
Better than once-upon-a-time. Real-life, coarse-ground
stories laced with ethnic spice and the requisite fat
encased in reverie to hold the narrative tight. Old jokes:

Hey, is that a knockwurst in your pocket or are you just
	happy to see me?
or long love: My father made a buttered Bologna sandwich
for my mother and brought it to her in bed every night
while she read.

Virtual Meets Reality:
The Story of the Magical Mystery Painting
For Aline

Il y avait une fois....

There was a time when technology ruled

People were connected by wire,

But a good story still held the people's ear,

Of a good story they'd never tire.

The following tale boasts an old plot

Of how two people once met,

A country apart, a twist of fate,

This hip tale stars the Internet.

Part I: The Coincidence

Meet Diane from Minnesota who

During a quick lunchtime stop,

Found a small oil painting of flowers

In a local consignment shop.

Aah, she said, it speaks to me,

It's primitive, the colors are bold

The flowers dance, the leaves emote,

I can't leave this painting here in the cold.

There was an artist's signature,

Which piqued her curiousity,

She logged onto the world-wide web

To search the artist's history.

To her surprise the closest hit
Came up Aline Martineau,
An artist "celebre" from Quebec
'Til then a name she didn't know.

Miss Diane, sensing a trail,
Phoned and e mailed a line,
Aline, a lover of mysteries, too,
Considered this inquiry just fine.

"Is it yours or isn't it?", Diane asked Aline,
"Probably not", the answer came,
"I don't remember painting it", still
The correspondence went on all the same.

Subjects moved to art and beyond,
Soon it became quite clear,
Though these two people had never met,
They functioned in a similar sphere.

Part II: The Decision
"Come to Quebec", Aline said,
Diane thought fast and said "oui,"
The stars at the time were directly aligned,
A meeting was nec-ess-ary.

On September 11, 2001, the old world
Changed over to the new.

A wave of terror covered the earth,
Diane didn't know what to do.

"Come", said Aline, "It will be fabulous.
Put aside, if you can, your fear,
Come to Quebec, let us meet face to face
The welcome committee waits for you here."

Part III: The Meeting
At the airport, Lesage it's called,
The rapport was instant and breezy,
Aline and Clement, her husband supreme,
Made the late night arrival so easy.

For the next three days, they walked and talked
Talked and walked and ate,
Up a thousand stairs, down the same,
Better than either could anticipate.

Through the haute ville et bas,
At the house on Rue St. Olivier,
Clement and Aline hosted Diane,
In a thoroughly marvelous way.

A cosmic aura floated over it all,
Casting a phosphorescent glow,
On the visit to Aline's atelier
And the poetry posters from Bordeaux.

Then when it came time to leave,
The goodbye was somewhat tough,
For only three days with Clement and Aline,
Were definitely not enough.

Epilogue
A tale of technology and fact,
Being neither myth nor fiction,
Requires a mystical element
To infuse poetic friction.

So when Diane returned home,
She consulted with a soothsayer
Who invoked the spirit of a past life,
In affirming an ancient layer.

The story ends here for now,
Proof that magic and mystery thrive
In the vibrant dust of everyday life
If you've the courage to leave the hive.

Resilience
For Anne who was there for every treatment

This morning it makes its appearance,
the bristle, a lone coarse hair,
spiky. Seen in bright sunlight
such a hair on the chin would invite the image
of every wicked witch from Hansel and Gretel
to Rapunzel . A human sprout, object of revulsion,
to be whisked, tweezed, waxed off right away.
But not today.

Today it stands like scrub
found after a firestorm or a weed
in the ashes of Hiroshima, white juices still running,
a plucky unplucked bugger
making a show of might and (de)spite,
one survivor of multiple rushes of toxins
scorch and strafe will not destroy.
Left there it has no choice; it can only
lean into the light.

Voltaire's* Fingers
"Mes doigts enfles, Monsieur, me refusent le plaisir de
vous ecrire de ma main."
(My swollen fingers, sir, do not permit me the pleasure
of writing to you with my own hand.
From a letter in the Voltaire Museum in Geneva)

These digits, once the extension of all thought,

gave life to my most elevated insights,

the banal, too, and the wit winnowed to satire

admired, and skewered, by so many.

Hobbled now, my hands sit on creaking knees

like stunned spiders, each spark postponed

until one scribe or another comes to gather my words

and cast them lightly across an open page.

I have not forgotten the scratch of quill

on fresh parchment, the outpouring of ideas,

what came as speedy execution or deliberate.

No longer mine the somersault of ciphers, they are

     his now,

the elation of seeing word on word, line on line—

his eye is the first to scan them, and he stifles his

     boredom

easily detected at every pause for comma or point.

I rail at this insult, this derailment. HA!

(Another jest destined to dissolve in air)

The head cannot do its work without the hand.

*Francois Marie Arouet deVoltaire (1694-1778), French philosopher
and author

The Days Before: A Monologue
Dedicated to the people whose magic and love got me
through the days before

Sitting on the passenger seat of my green Ford Focus is a
packet of the world's most photographed left breast. Mine.
Mammograms and ultrasound images being transported on
a rush run to the surgeon who will study them and do a biopsy based on his reading of these mysterious shadows and
clouds with my name on them. This is no longer my breast.
Disconnected, it could be an arm, a leg, a testicle.
I review what brought me to this point.

Day 1:

In the middle of doing a series of Vietnamese exercises
taught to me by the aged aunt of a friend of mine, I find a
lump in my left breast. Nah, I say. It's just another one of
those hummocks in a line of mini- mountain ranges on the
side of my chest detected and ignored for many years. Besides, it hurts. Malignant lumps don't hurt, they say. But I
go back to the spot. It haunts me, feels different. It is different. This is no hummock; it is a lump. I let it go for a week.
Don't panic, the articles on this subject advise. I don't. I ig-
nore it instead. Maybe it will disappear. I drink less coke, cut
down on chocolate. No change. I phone to make an appointment to get it checked .

Day 4:

The OB/GYN, whom I have never met before, is handsome, not too far from my age. The last thing most women

want in this situation at this time is a good-looking male doctor, but I have been assigned to one. I focus on his expensive pima cotton green and white tattersall -checked shirt, light-starched fresh from the laundry, firm press on the sleeve. (Good textile distraction). He is noncommittal, honest about his doubt. "You have a palpable mass. It requires a closer look." He refers me to a radiology group. I am stunned. I had expected to be dismissed.

The confirmed mass and I are plenty happy to see daylight. Outside in the parking lot, I meet Roger, a friend from my writer's group. We regard each other with the unasked question any two people would have in the parking lot of Health Partners: What are **you** here for? It takes only a second and no urging from him to blurt out my news. He is quiet, calming, tells me other lump stories that end well. This is the first of many stories of this kind. The "I found a lump and it was only a cyst happy ending" story.

Day 7:

I spend two hours at the radiologist's office. Images one after another are taken while many others, mostly bad, form in my mind. I am impatient. Finally, I am able to watch the ultrasound images on the monitor. I see a foggy wash of gray and there, on the screen, the dark irregular shape. My innards as CNN.

The technician taking the ultrasound is young, the first friendly face for a while. She suggests that the black Rorschach- looking ink blot on the monitor looks okay- not "ugly" like the bad ones. I breathe with relief.

Optimism is replaced quickly by the radiologist who comes in and peers at the screen. He studies. "It needs a biopsy", he says seriously, very seriously. I sink on the table. "Do you understand? It needs a biopsy". I begin to understand all right. I hear the words condensed to the essential message. He believes it is a malignancy. He says straight out that it is suspicious. He offers to do the biopsy then and there. I can't. I need air and a conversation with the referring physician. I refuse and stumble out.

All these details are dumped in the hallway of my friends' Anita's and Tom's house a few blocks away. Sit, Anita says. I can't. A cup of chamomile tea, she offers. I can't. The powder-sugared lemon cake she has prepared sits on the kitchen counter. She is an artist on paper and in the kitchen as well. I know I am missing something good. I can't. I pace back and forth like a panther.

She suggests a walk. It is the right antidote for this restless, angry behavior. The November evening is mild. The old houses in the neighborhood reflect the last yellow light. The visual distraction calms me down. We talk about the bad possibilities and the good. She is firm, doesn't let me run ahead too far, urges me to get to the surgeon quickly. She reminds me that there is no final diagnosis yet. I forget how assertive she can be.

Day 8:

I call the doctor who referred me (the handsome one). "Make your appointment for the biopsy", he tells me. "Call the surgeon." I set it up quickly. All this is happening quickly. I need time to chew and mull. No one is offering time. Receptionists are making instant appointments. I am to go in two days later.

Day 9:

The surgeon I am assigned to is the long-time friend of old and very close friends of mine, who are both physicians themselves. I notify them instantly of the coincidence, amazed at the happy accident. I feel better already. Not so isolated and alone. My friend calls and tells the surgeon that I am coming over for a biopsy.

Day 10:

In the waiting room of the surgery office, a Hmong family is sitting. There are two parents and a small boy about four or five. The father is reading a magazine. The child pulls away the magazine and hands the father a children's book he has chosen from a pile on a nearby table. He climbs on the father's lap and together they look at the book, laugh and go through the pages one by one, the boy narrating each page in Hmong. It is an intimate act, a tribute to the father's delight in his child and to their closeness. I want to save the scene and describe it to my colleagues as a fine example of how literacy acts take place in an immigrant family. For the first time in days I think about my long-time work with refugees and feel plugged in to life at the office. I wonder which member of the family is going to have surgery.

My name is called. I enter the inner offices. The X Rays are lit up on the wall. The surgeon, looks closely, examining the shadows and the ink blot. "It looks very questionable," he says. "We'll test today with a biopsy; results will be back tomorrow."

That ink blot (out out damn spot) can't belong to me. I don't do cancer. I have plans. I stop hoping. Two negative reactions from doctors thus far make a positive; that's simple mathematics. My husband and I squeeze each other's hand. This is a first for us.

I lay quietly through the "procedure", the harvesting of tissue. The trick is to focus on the wall. The very kind surgeon and nurse keep asking ,"Are you all right?" I am. This is easy. It's real stuff, not the anxiety, worry and doubt that is unknown and crazy-making.

Day 11:
Today we find out the results of the biopsy at 1:00. I am to meet my husband at the surgeon's office a few minutes before. I approach the medical center and decide to do what Reginald Perrin does, *disappear.* I drive around the same block five times. I simply won't go in. I wonder how it would be to disappear. Take off my clothes and walk into the ocean. That is *The Best of British Comedy,* this is not. I

imagine this, stiffen my spine and park the car. The fantasy alone settles me down. It offers a dramatic sidestep for me to chuckle over.

The results are confirmed positive. No shilly shallying. My choices are presented : big cuts, smaller cuts, testing lymph nodes , blue dye injections, inpatient, out patient, the if's, the notion that nothing is certain until the doctors go in and have a look. About a third of these facts register. My husband captures the other two thirds. I plead for a few days to breathe and get ready. Unlike others who are eager to get each step over with, I want time to process what is happening. I leave the office with a surgery date a week away and a very large pile of pamphlets and videos to review.

I return home, put the pile on the stairs and begin the process of informing the few people who are waiting to hear the results. It is selective this list of people you let in on the events and your fear. You don't want to alarm them, but you have to tell some people for your own sanity and because they are in your closest circle and want to know what is going on. This is the group who buffers you in the days before. They cry, call, make time, listen, cook, nudge, indulge, advise where necessary and walk you, literally, walk you around many corners.

Days 12-18: I can't get enough communication and contact. I don't want to be alone. These are the days of good advice, the answering machine, comforts and the coping plan.

The Good Advice: Sage words caught in a net:

You have to get used to the idea. (eldest son)

You need courage. I did it. You can do this. (cancer survivor in the office)

Postpone surgery? Bad idea. You speak to <u>me</u> before you make that decision. (doctor friend)

Now starts the time when *you* become the caretaker for those around you.

(cancer survivor colleague who had the disease at an early age)

Are you kidding? Die of this? You won't die of this. It's your blood pressure that will get you in the end! (pharmacist friend)

I'll cook. You'll eat. (friend)

Do nothing? No treatment? I have seen metastasized breast cancer, and it isn't pretty. You won't like it. (doctor friend)

Sit back and let us do the driving from now on. (the surgeon)

You're putting in the time now to buy time at the other end. (friend)

Level with your (adult) children about what you're going through. Don't hide your feelings from them and don't exclude them. (a young coworker)

I figure I have a week to live before my life changes. I set out to have a good time- play, meet friends, eat, write, walk, watch films, be distracted as much and as often as possible.

The Answering Machine records constantly.

Hi, Diane, it's --------- checking to see how you are. Thinking of you. Call me.

Diane, we're going to the country for the weekend (First call). Second call: we won't go if you need us. Third call: do you want to come with us and relax by the lake?"

Hey, Diane, you may be okay, but what about *me*? I have to cope with this information too.

Je te souhaite bon courage, Diane.

Bad, biddleboppin bad, bummer, fuck, shit. SHIT.

Hi, Diane, how are you doing? The baby is sick, H just lost his job and there's a spot on my mother's lung. But I don't want to depress you.

Hey, Diane, my sister's brother-in-law's aunt's cousin's twin had the same experience as you—no evidence picked up on a recent mammogram.

Mom, I'm coming home. Be in the night before surgery. Flight 438 at 5:56. Pick me up at Door 1. Let's go for dinner on the way home.

Sistah, we don't have cancer in the family, craziness yes, but not cancer. How can this be?

The sources of comfort become clear:

Large doses of Vietnamese food

Weeping anywhere with anyone

Walking

Not too many questions

Not too many scary stories of any kind

Not too much information on radiation or chemotherapy treatment

Quiet people who listen

Pretending that things are normal

Jokes and funny people

Distractions, distractions, and more distractions

The Strategy:

I design my coping plan. Everyday I am to do three
things:

1. Complain vigorously, kick and scream, rage at the
wind

2. Hear an uplifting story, preferably inspirational

3. Hear something funny

This course of action will get me through. Friends and
family are enlisted. My illness becomes a community project. Everyone wants to help and to be there. One will do
jokes, one meals, one, video runs, one walks. The support
and kindness, the generosity are overwhelming. The distractions make life seem as it always was, just a lot more in-
tense. I sober up, calm down and get ready for surgery. The
plans I was so worried about become irrelevant. I do, indeed, finally *get used to the idea*. I finally understand that I
have cancer, and the point, simply put, is to be rid of it as
quickly as possible.

John P. Pikala

John Pikala makes his home in north Minneapolis with his life partner Cristopher. Besides doing his damnedest to develop a regular writing practice, John enjoys walking and biking. John also gets pleasure from cooking and having friends and family for dinner, attending live theater, and going to the movies and watching films at home.

The Fifties in Northeast Minneapolis

1953: Home and Family

My childhood home on Twelfth Avenue, initially covered in faux brick, was given a face lift in the early Fifties and survived about forty more years with an exterior of broad, white asbestos shingles that concealed its original tar paper "Depression siding." As an eight-year old, I loved our house, though I now realize how very plain it was, especially when compared to the Churillas' across the driveway to the west, a house built with real bricks and whose front boasted three, two-story fluted Ionic columns. The front steps of our house were crumbling, our lot was extremely narrow, the house on our east side stood barely six feet away, and we had no garage—the driveway belonged to the Greek revival house. But, on the other hand, nobody in our family had a car then, so we had no need for a garage. And besides, delicate lilies of the valley bloomed in the shade of our house on the rear (north) side; lush ferns thrived in the cool darkness between the two too-close-together houses; Grandma's peppermint and rhubarb plants and her raspberry bushes produced tasty treats year after year; and downstairs in Grandma and Grandpa's, the living and sitting rooms had floors with ornamental inlaid wood designs as well as elegant wooden piers that provided a passage between the rooms.

But the most delightful features of our house were the two screened-in front porches, one upstairs, one down. It is true that the Churillas also had front porches, but theirs were not protected against all the bugs that swarmed during every Minnesota summer. Behind our screens, I'd sit with Grandma and Grandpa, keeping them company on their downstairs porch, and listen to their conversations with the neighbors who passed by our house on the way to Sampson's Grocery Store, Lazaar's Liquors, the Northeast Bakery, or Lucille's Flower Shop.

In the upstairs porch, my four-year old sister Patti and I would pass summer days playing Chutes and Ladders, Candy Land, and Go to the Dump; my friends and I would read comic books and work on our stamp collections; and Mom would make pitchers of cherry or grape Kool Aid for us to enjoy in our aerie. A maroon couch had been demoted to the front porch when Mom and Dad got a new sofa for the living room. We'd loll on the old couch and watch the daytime action in the street, and at night we'd ask Mom to "work her magic." Only she knew how to lift the couch's long seat in such a way that it would release its catch and lower the back, and—*Voilá*—the couch was now a double bed. How our parents determined who would get to sleep on the porch—they or us kids—I don't remember; but when it was our turn, how refreshing it was to experience the cool breezes in those pre-air conditioning July and August nights!

During the day, we'd lower the thick, striped canvas shades—inside the porches, both upstairs and down—to keep out the summer sun. The shades had small metal rings sewn on the backs, through which passed wires that were attached to the lintels and the sills. This system kept the shades close to the screens and prevented them from flapping wildly when we had closed them against a summer thunderstorm.

Every spring the porches needed a thorough scrubbing—ceiling, shades, screens, and floor. It was customary to wash away the accumulated winter grime by hosing everything down and letting the water pour out the four spouts at the base of the walls—two in front and one on each side. Mom would use a rope to pull up the garden hose and then would spray away—sometimes for as long as half an hour—until the spouts spewed clear water. Later that day or the next, Grandma would use the hose on her porch.

In the spring of 1953, and who now remembers why, Mom and her mother-in-law were not speaking to each other. One morning, Grandma unilaterally decided to clean her porch; she hosed it down in the usual way and then placed on the porch all her usual furniture. Well, not speaking was one thing, but changing the pattern of the spring ritual was well beyond what Mom thought reasonable. "What the holy hell does that woman think she's doing? Who does she think she is? Does she think we're going to spend the whole summer with a dirty porch?" And so, Mom made up her mind not only to clean our porch in the usual way but also to say nothing about it to Grandma. When all that black, filthy water began running down into the porch below, we heard Grandma run through the hallway and onto her porch, yelling in Slovak and cursing in English. It was not uncommon for her to use Slovak, even though she was born in America and was very proud of her unaccented

English, but for her to use coarse language was an occasion indeed—this was the first and only time I heard *hell* and *damn* come out of her mouth. It took a couple weeks of cooling off before mother-in-law and daughter-in-law ended their squabble and for us kids to feel comfortable about spending time on either porch.

Except for that one episode, relations between us upstairs and my grandparents and uncle downstairs were more than warm; we all were a family together. Holiday dinners alternated between downstairs and up. Mom's and Grandma's summer canning always occurred on the same days—both houses would be redolent of vinegar when beets and cukes were being put up, bread and butter pickles brought the added smell of turmeric, and the aroma of stewed tomatoes and spicy tomato sauce came from both kitchens at the same time later in the year. Only Grandma canned peaches and rhubarb sauce, so I'd go downstairs to enjoy their sweet, fruity perfumes. There was a rhythm to our lives in Northeast Minneapolis, and the yearly tempo came to its culmination at Christmas time.

If our uncle had asked Mom and Dad, "Can this matted cotton 'beard'; this stiff, scratchy, fabric mask of a merry man with rosy cheeks; and this too-tight red suit, again this year, held together with safety pins—can this costume really fool the kids,"—our parents would have answered yes. It was true: year after year my sister and I willingly believed that the guest in our house every December 24th really was Santa Claus, come in person to give us gifts we knew we could not have earned. But even this year, with the brandy and Dutch Masters cigars on Santa's breath stronger than ever, Uncle Pete was not exposed as an imposter. "Saint Nick is an adult, isn't he?" we kids reasoned. "Adults smoke and drink, don't they?" And so we continued to be willing participants in the yearly holiday fantasy.

This Christmas Eve, as expected, Dad was using his 16-mm Revere movie camera to record our appreciation of the presents Santa was handing out to us. This was the model that required several hundred candlepower's worth of movie lights to capture anything on film. Dad aimed the camera and blazing light bar at Patti and me, and, knowing the drill, we turned on our movie star smiles and waved our movie star hands. With all the Christmas tree lights burning—more this year than ever before—as well as with almost all the other lights on in our house, the draw on electricity was just too much for the building's ancient wiring, and we blew a fuse.

"*YAY-zhush! Ma-RI-ah!*" Unbelievably, we were hearing Santa Claus speak in Slovak to invoke the help of Jesus and Mary! Santa had never before used the language Uncle Pete used so often. Before anyone could say jingle bells, Santa abruptly began to shout his "Ho, Ho, Ho's," said it was time for him to visit the homes of the neighbor kids, admonished us to be good until his return next year, and vanished down the pitch-black front stairs.

A couple minutes later, Uncle Pete came back from his every-Christmas-Eve cigar-buying trip to Dady's Drug Store—right on time to replace the burnt out fuse. What a happy coincidence that Uncle Pete had returned just then, Patti and I said to each other, wanting to open our presents and see what we got. Once the lights were back on, we began to tear the ribbons and paper off the packages, Uncle Pete sat down in a cloud of cigar smoke, and Dad handed him a Christian Brothers brandy and water.

While my sister and I were exclaiming over our presents, I didn't have an inkling that I would soon begin to interpret all the "Uncle Pete clues" that had always been there for me to discern. Moving from gift to gift, I didn't know that some four months hence a classmate would convince me there was no Santa Claus. No, at that moment, I was grateful for the visit of that right jolly old elf. "Look at all this loot! We *must* have been as good as Santa said we were!"

1956: Family and Friends

Eighteen days before Christmas, every year, on "Pearl Harbor Day," my birthday arrived. Birthdays were big deals for us kids in northeast Minneapolis. Invitations were sent out in the mail, the house was decorated with balloons and crepe paper streamers, the dining room table was adorned with a paper birthday tablecloth, and there were matching napkins and paper plates. In 1956, I turned twelve....

Mom is tying her babushka around my eyes. It's the tattered headscarf she wears when she vacuums the house, scrubs the kitchen floor, and washes the back steps—a fringed, gray-purple square of fabric, dotted with tiny pale yellow and pink flowers. The scarf smells of Avon and sweat.

She twirls me around by my shoulders to disorient me before my attempt to pin the tail on the donkey. My pant legs are too short, the waist too high, and my plaid shirt has very long collar points. I'm giggling like a girl as I spin around. Standing around me, my friends, too, are laughing. When I stop, I extend my right hand, trying to pin the paper donkey tail at least on a wall, if not on the donkey's butt. I do make it to a wall and in fact stick the tail on the donkey's belly. I won't be the one to win a prize, though. Even if I had exactly targeted the donkey's rear end, Mom's rules ensure that the birthday boy does not get a prize; only guests can receive prizes.

Here at the party are Jerry Genosky, Tommy Plantenberg, Tony Lynch, Bobby Koniar, Gloria Jean Stasek, Patty Samek, and Barbara Rabatin—all are in the seventh grade with me at St. Cyril's School. Skinny Jerry, with light brown hair, buck teeth, and glasses, wears a thin, long-sleeved, striped sport shirt and baggy brown corduroys. The only classmate besides Jerry to wear glasses is Tommy, and his glasses are so thick and make his eyes look so much larger than they are, that the eyeglasses are his most prominent feature. He's the bulkiest boy at the party—stocky, solid, and strong. Tommy's dad, Ray, drives a truck for Raymond Transfer, and I think it's cool that Raymond is working for Raymond.

Tony is only slightly less skinny than Jerry. He looks like a farm boy, olive-complected and with longish hair slicked back on his head and parted on the left, and he's almost always smiling. Tony has a tremendous appetite and will later eat three pieces of birthday cake. Next year at Many Point Scout Camp, I'll share a tent with him and find out he's a bed-wetter. My best friend Bobby and I have just recently discovered that we both have a vocation to the priesthood and plan to enter the seminary after grade school. Bobby will die of rheumatic fever in the spring of our eighth grade year. His will be the second death I encounter; Grandpa Pikala had died of a heart attack when I was ten. I'll cry for days, not understanding or accepting why God had to take Bobby.

Though back then boys sometimes came to birthday parties sporting ties or at least with their top shirt button buttoned, the girls always dressed up, and Patty, Barbara, and Gloria Jean are wearing colorful party dresses and patent leather shoes.

Once we finish with pin the tail on the donkey, Mom gets us going in bobbing for apples, dropping clothespins in the bottle, and playing "Twenty Questions." She makes sure that everyone will go home with a prize.

Dad captures all the activities on film. In addition to my friends, my sister Patti and three-year old brother Jimmy are also at the party; they need little prompting to mug for the camera.

Finally it's time for our family's traditional birthday lunch of "party spaghetti"—elbow macaroni, ground beef, tomato sauce, some chopped onions and celery, a bit of allspice, and a little salt and pepper—potato chips, pickles, lime Jell-O, and strawberry Kool Aid. The highlight of the meal is the made-from-scratch cherry nut cake, frosted pink, and served with vanilla ice cream. My friends pick up the tune from Mom and sing the song of the day, with Jerry, as usual, doing his imitation of a dog baying at the moon, "Happy birthday to youuu. Happy birthday to youuuu...." I succeed in one try at blowing out all twelve candles, and then it's on to my presents. [I'm imagining that it is on this one birthday that I receive all the gifts I treasured in child-hood.]

First I unwrap an electric wood-burning set, about which I'll later hear Uncle Pete say, "Don't burn the house down, *Yohnko* [Johnny]." But I'm excited now because none of my friends have one, and the boys start talking about all the signboards I'll be making with my new wood-burner.

Next is a kit for making an antique copper reproduction of "The Famous Last Supper" painting, a copy of which hangs in school. My friends don't really appreciate this gift, but Grandma will later tell me that she is eager for me to complete the project, which she knows will be beautiful. The kit includes one large rectangular sheet of copper; a slightly smaller plastic form embossed with the Last Supper scene; a pointed, hard plastic tool for working the copper so that the scene is, as it were, transferred from plastic to copper; and a bottle of antiquing fluid that will make an "authentic-looking final product, suitable for framing." The label on the bottle warns that a parent should supervise when the liquid is applied.

169

But the biggest and best of all gifts is my very own chemistry set. Having seen so many mad scientist movies, I had begged my parents for the tools and equipment I would need to go along with my imaginary white lab coat. And here it is! I hear from all around me, "Ooh"; "Wow"; "Golly"; "Gee!" I know this is the big one! This is the hinged, double-sided, five rows to a side, six bottles to a row chemistry set. Here are 60 little bottles of white and yellow powders, clear and milky fluids, brown and reddish crystals. One bottle even has liquid silver inside, mercury! An accompanying box contains glass test tubes and flexible tubes and corks and metal holders. "And it's mine, I tell you. All mine. They called me mad at the university." Oh yes, I had the lingo down. Uncle Pete will later say, "Don't blow the house up, Johnny." But Mom, smiling, now says, "It is what you wanted, isn't it?"

My heart's desire was indeed granted; I was delighted with my presents and happy as well to be gifted with good friends and a loving family.

But while home, family, and friends were extremely important in the Fifties, we recognized one institution as more indispensable than all the others; we viewed that institution not so much as an organization, but as a parent—"Mother Church."

1954 and 1958: The Church

In preparation for First Holy Communion at Ss. Cyril and Methodius Catholic Church, the nuns instructed my class for weeks on the Baltimore Catechism:

"Who made the world?" —"God made the world."

"Who is God?" —"God is the Creator of heaven and earth and all things."

We memorized the Act of Contrition and the preface that was to begin our confession of sins: "Bless me, Father, for I have sinned. It has been [so many weeks, months, or whatever span of time] since my last confession"; or, for this initial confessing, "This is my first confession." Whatever the introduction we spoke in the confessional, next was to come the recitation of our sins.

How much evil could a nine-year old do? Disobeying Mom, fighting with my sister, letting a friend copy my math homework. The Roman Catholic Church recognized seven years old as the Age of Reason, of being able to tell right from wrong, of being capable of committing mortal sins. And, to be ready for my First Communion, I not only had to wear a white shirt, symbolic of my spotless soul, and tie, indicative of the formality of the occasion, but I also had to be pure of heart—free of the "taint of sin." That meant owning up to all my moral failings, being truly sorry for them, and asking for and receiving absolution from the priest. The solemn occasion also required believing that the wafer—that I would soon discover tasted exactly like the fish food I sprinkled into my aquarium—was indeed the Body of Christ.

171

Confession. Absolution. Transubstantiation. All this was pretty perplexing stuff for us fourth graders. Would we—could we—really embrace all these practices? Certainly! We were aware of no alternative, for these were the beliefs of our community. The School Sisters of Notre Dame taught and our parish priests preached truths that were reliable and a faith that provided certainty. The community didn't question; we felt no ambiguity; we had no cause to doubt. The Koniars, the Plantenbergs, the Rabatins, the Slotaskis, the Churillas, the Genoskys, the Pikalas—the lives of us all in the Northeast Minneapolis Catholic "ghetto" were anchored in our neighborhood church. Weddings, funerals, retreats, parish missions, baptisms, festivals, anniversary parties—all these occurred, or at least began, in St. Cyril's. Consequently, while the concepts the nuns were teaching us in fourth grade remained baffling, all we kids had to do was accept. We had only to yield to the sisters' wisdom and devotion, to go along with the centuries-old traditions of the Church. We didn't have to understand or even believe, try though we may. It was quite simple, really. All that was asked of us was to participate in the process.

So on a warm May Sunday in 1954, I was putting on a tie for the first time—a clip-on tie. I was about to take a big step toward adulthood in my community.

That feeling of being part of a community and of the certainty of our Catholic beliefs endured throughout the Fifties and was typified by Forty Hours Devotion, observed annually at the Church of St. Cyril. The Forty Hours rituals of 1958 ended, as they all did, with a grand procession of nearly the entire parish community.

We all are gathered in the church basement, and the excitement is palpable. The choir are all dressed in their best clothes, quietly chatting in Slovak and English. The nuns—there's Sister Mary Imelda, my teacher—are lining up by grade almost all the school kids, except for me and some of the other eighth grade boys, grandly superior to the rest by virtue of being vested in altar boy cassocks and surplices. All the priests, who have come from their own parishes to participate in the concluding event of St. Cyril's celebration, are arrayed in their own cassocks and, some of them, in frilly, lacy, and very sheer surplices.

Father Ballent, our priest, gives the signal: it's time for everyone to find their places. Four men from the parish's Slovak Catholic Fraternal Association, looking more serious than any of the other adults, walk together to where a canopy, loosely folded up, is leaning. They take up the poles and lift them high, then spread themselves out and thereby unfurl the—"Oohhhh," everyone gasps—canopy which is ornamented with delicate rose, yellow, and jade flowers, and fringed with heavy gold tassels. The canopy is, of course, part of the last "unit" in the procession. The altar boy swinging the censer takes his place immediately in front of this moving tent. Before him, all the visiting priests; before them, the six altar boys carrying "torches," poles with red-glass-enclosed candles swinging on top; next, as many adults as want to walk in the procession, most moving their

173

fingers over the beads of their rosaries; then, all the school children grouped class by class with the nuns who are their teachers; almost at the front, the choir and its director, who will sing "Tantum, ergo, Sacramentum" ["So great a Sacrament"] and "O Salutaris Hostia" ["O Saving Victim"]; and leading the entire procession is the tallest altar boy carrying the ceremonial cross, flanked on either side by an acolyte.

Everyone is ready, a stillness comes upon us all, and there, way back at the end of the line, at the culmination of the procession, is the reason for it all: Father Ballent, now wearing an elaborate cape over his shoulders and down his arms and around his hands, grasps a golden monstrance, holds it high, and moves to his place between the four dignified men, the canopy offering protection and honor to what the priest carries. In the monstrance, displayed for all to see and worship, is a consecrated host, the Body of Christ, the Holiest of Holies. The procession solemnly mounts the stairs from the basement and into the church where every candle is ablaze. The altar boy swinging the censer really has his work cut out for him now, because he is walking backwards, facing the monstrance, and directing the billowing incense towards the host. As the monstrance passes by the faithful in their pews, they go down on their knees—there's Grandma, wearing her babushka and praying her rosary.

The procession moves up and down the aisles of the church, and the various units find their places—the choir in the loft, school children and adults in the front and back pews, respectively. When the torch bearers reach the sanctuary, they kneel on the first step leading to the high altar, three on each side. I'm there—the middle altar boy on the right. The clergy position themselves at individual priedieus facing the high altar. Our pastor slowly ascends the steps until he reaches the lofty platform on which the altar rests.

There is genuflecting, more incense, singing, bowing, even more incense, and—abruptly—silence. High up on the altar platform, Father Ballent, the only person in church not kneeling, turns to face the congregation, raises the monstrance even higher, and makes the sign of the cross with it over us all. We have just experienced Benediction of the Blessed Sacrament. Together now, everyone in the church recites the Divine Praises: "Blessed be God. Blessed be His holy name. Blessed be Jesus Christ, true God and true man. Blessed be the name of Jesus. Blessed be.... Blessed be.... Blessed be...." Finally, the choir leads us all in singing, "Holy God, we praise Thy name"....

Coda

A few weeks later, in June 1958, I graduated from St. Cyril's Grade School; and in October, Mom, Dad, Pat, Jim, and I moved to our new home near Lake Harriet. Grandma believed that my parents, filled with delusions of grandeur, were abandoning their simple origins in "nordeast" and also that she would never see us again. "It must be pretty nice to be moving in with the rich folks. Is that 'Linden Hills' area really in Minneapolis? *I've* never heard of it."

We did, of course, go back to visit Grandma and Uncle Pete, and they visited us as well. But in another, spiritual way, I have never been able to return to the neighborhood of

175

my youth. Even before my recent discovery that my childhood home on Twelfth Avenue had been torn down, I knew that I could not reclaim either the steadfast sense of community or the genuine simplicity that characterized my earlier life.

Part of me knows that in today's uneasy world my task is to attain my own sense of peace and security. But another part of me yearns for the assurance and certainty I experienced in the Fifties in Northeast Minneapolis.

Kate Smith

Trained in chemistry and business, and employed in corporate America as a scientist, marketer and manager, I've been a closet-writer since my early teens. Over the years, the idiosyncrasies of daily life intertwined with the exquisite flavors of travel on six continents have compelled me to write as a means to clarify my own thoughts on the similarities and paradoxes of *homo sapiens* and the societies we create. I am currently completing *Whispered Prophecy*, a novel about two siblings who as adults are destined to rule the highly complex and well-ordered Incan Empire. When they learn of a secret legend, their choices affect an entire civilization.

My Mother-in-Law, Jeanette

"Why did you get so tall?" Jeanette's petite mother complained with the same surprise and distaste of discovering sour milk.

"Now, Mother," her father responded, "You've raised a strong, healthy child who has become a lovely young lady. She simply inherited the height of my family and the beauty of yours."

"Well, I wish she'd had the good sense to leave the height for her brother." Her mother returned to her needlework with a sigh mixed with resignation and disgust. In 1932 at age fifteen, Jeanette was a slender, 5'9" teenager who looked completely uncomfortable with her newly acquired stature. Her eyes pleaded for forgiveness as she stood before her parents. With a barely perceptible nod, her father reassured her as he signaled her to leave. Relieved, she turned to gracelessly tip toe up the stairs to the sanctuary of her room.

Years later, Jeanette often recounted this vignette for her own children, who as adults ranged in height from 5' 10" to 6'5". She chuckled at her mother's assumption that she had grown to spite her, and yet she still seemed uncomfortable with her own height. I first heard her tell the story shortly after I married her youngest son, Dan. When I was fifteen, I too had reached my adult height, an unimpressive 5'2", and as I heard the story, I couldn't imagine why anyone would reject such strength and physical presence. Of course, I'd never had to contend with ducking under doorsills, cramping feet in a bed with tightly tucked blankets, or sitting in an airplane seat with my knees pressed against the next seat. Even so, it seemed better than being unable to see over the dashboard or having cold feet because the chair cut off the blood to my dangling legs. It was another thirty years before I could answer her mother's question.

Jeanette often retold other snippets of her childhood in western Pennsylvania that in her memory was a small piece of heaven. Fondly she described the joy of being rewarded with a penny to take to the corner store where it bought enough ginger candy to share with a friend for a week. And she loved the hikes in the mountains with her father who always carried a walking stick with a brass tip for killing copperheads. Many times she spoke of her father's love for art and the beautiful wood carvings he sculpted from off-cut lumber and tree knots they found on their walks. These became treasured gifts for his wife and are now proudly displayed by his descendants.

She never expressed any rancor when she described her childhood in a vanished world, although it wasn't always carefree. Every week her mother, with Jeanette's help of course, washed, bleached, starched and ironed every bed sheet and curtain in the house to keep pace with the ubiquitous coal ash. Among her other chores, she was taught at a young age to remove every collar before washing and then sew it back in place. Although safety pins were readily available, the punishment was harsh for choosing to use them instead of a thread and needle. Likewise, she learned she didn't like the taste of soap after she repeated, without understanding, something she heard her older brother say, "H- E- double toothpicks!"

Added to her childhood stories, Jeanette freely repeated a host of favorite episodes about her own children. For example, there was the persnickety neighbor who initiated a conversation over the backyard fence just as she finished weeding the garden. Not wanting to hear of the perceived misdeeds of her children or engage in the local gossip, she carefully examined the dirt still lodged under her nails and cuticles before responding, "Sorry, I can't stay; it's time to knead the bread dough. It's the best way to get out the dirt, you know." In the same crafty manner, she didn't offer an explanation to the disapproving minister who had a habit of making unannounced visits. The minister drank several cups of coffee and recited Bible verses as he stole glances at the brightly colored orbs dotting the twelve foot high living room ceiling. The boys had discovered that if they rubbed a balloon on their hair and jumped toward the ceiling, the static would carry and hold it there for a week or more. She felt no obligation to justify her family to a minister who deemed it necessary to make spot inspections.

One of Jeanette's favorite memories arose when her tallest sons, now young men, returned home on a snowy evening. From the kitchen window she watched them gradually unfold as they extracted themselves from the car in the driveway. The elder carefully held a rumpled tea towel on his extended hand. Curious, she met the "boys" at the door. "Ma, you're not going to like this," he offered as he unfolded the towel. "It's for Marie." Curled into a tiny ball, a pure white kitten lay asleep in his hand. Never having lived with a pet, she wasn't pleased, but couldn't refuse the gift her sons brought for her only daughter. For days she followed the cat around the house as it explored its new domain. She grew to love that cat and the others that followed.

For Jeanette, the church and girl scouts were central interests, and children were paramount. Her family of giants was quiet, congenial and always well-mannered. By comparison, my family consisted of two parents and seven hyper-active, loud, quarrelsome children. After what seemed like raising my three younger siblings and babysitting for others through college, I had no further interest in children. Furthermore, I was convinced the human population should decline, another reason to avoid motherhood. Even more contrary to my mother-in-law's interests, I considered the church, any church, to be one of man's worst inventions. My father was the son of a missionary and my mother a devout Bible reader. Even before my teens, I was disgusted with the church, but was required to attend. After dating the preacher's son and getting the inside scoop, I was completely disillusioned and actively explored other Christian sects as well as the great religions of the world. I discovered their remarkable similarities, and I rejected them all. Considering our vastly different interests, what could I possibly have in common with this woman?

For years I simply watched and listened to Jeanette, offering only scant information when directly asked. In my family, such divergent opinions were tinder for a fight; I had no desire to create trouble with my mother-in-law, and I never did. It was years before I learned that in the sixties she became a member of NOW, an organization I considered too radical to join. Decades passed before I knew she researched the lessons before teaching women's Bible classes. She put the scripture in the temporal context of the author and compared it to the contemporary controversies in the church; she didn't simply teach the text according to the prescribed dogma. It was thirty years and after her husband's death before I learned that he had approached her shortly after they were married and told her who she should vote for. She promptly informed him that she listened to the radio and read the papers; she didn't need his help. Although she led an apparently conventional life, she was a feisty, self-determined woman with a far-reaching curiosity that propelled her well ahead of her time. I guess we weren't so different after all.

In spite of my own convictions, what I cherished most about "Ma Smith", as I came to call her, was her unaffected, unlimited, and unconditional love for her children, grandchildren and great grandchildren. Never did I hear her interfere with the childrearing of her grandchildren. Even when they were whiny, sugar-hyped brats to the point that I wanted to spank them, she quietly encouraged the parents and went on about her business. Of course her behavior also demanded that I develop my tolerance and self-control; no doubt I am a better person for knowing her. Through their bad relationships, divorces, unorthodox educational choices, suicide and a host of other difficulties, she always greeted her children with her immutable love. In the same way, anyone her children brought into her life was welcomed and accepted. It didn't matter what they looked like, what country they called home, or what they might have done. Since she was not only a storyteller, but an avid listener, she invariably drew them into a conversation with a pertinent, but never invasive question. If the newcomer hesitated, she often smiled and added, "I'm interested," as she patiently waited for the stranger to feel at ease. After all these years I still stand in grateful disbelief that she extended that same love to me.

I had only recently realized that when I visited her at the nursing home where she was recuperating from a serious staph infection on a dreary Wednesday in December. Even in her morphine-induced sleep she appeared to be in pain, but, as she requested, I woke her whenever I arrived. After affectionate greetings, she asked her usual question in between breaths, "So what ... have you ... been doing ... today?"

Happy to entertain her with the mundane, I prattled on, "The holiday party for the people Dan works with is Saturday. This morning I made lasagna for the buffet and started putting up decorations. Tomorrow I'll clean the house and do some more cooking."

"Sounds wonderful. Is your ... Christmas tree ... up yet?"

"No it takes up too much room during the party and besides, we'll be in Las Vegas next week. I'd rather not have a tree in the house while we're gone."

"That's smart." The oxygen tube needed adjusting, so she let go of my hand, moved the tube to make it more comfortable, grimaced as she adjusted herself in her chair, and breathed deeply as she again reached for my hand.

Hoping to distract her I asked, "How was your physical therapy today?"

"I did ... all the ... weight lifting ... with my arms ... and my legs," she responded in short clips. "She wanted ... me to walk ... afterwards. I couldn't ... even stand. My legs ... were jello." Tears welled up in her eyes.

"You walked yesterday; you're just tired," I tried to reassure her. "Maybe tomorrow will be better. Will she let you walk before you lift the weights?"

"No. She says ... I need ... to build ... my strength. Walking ... only second." She paused to catch her breath after the exertion of speaking. "She thinks ... I'm a ... wimp."

"You're not a wimp; you've just been ill and need to rebuild your muscles. Be patient, you were really sick. It'll take time to recover."

Her tired eyes looked to me for reassurance, but finally she admitted, "It hurts. No matter ... what I do, I hurt." She wasn't looking for sympathy, just a kind word. In spite of years of suffering with arthritis, bouts of gall bladder trouble and breast cancer, she never complained. Even then she didn't look frail, but the suffering had exhausted her.

"You'll feel better soon," I said with a smile and as much confidence as my honesty allowed.

We sat quietly while I tried to warm her perpetually cold hands and she told me about one of the other residents playing the songs of her college years on the piano. Unashamed, she cried as she told me how she wept to hear them again and to remember playing the same songs with her friends on the piano in the parlor. "Oh what ... fun ...we had!" Her body shook with her tears and gasping breath. "They're all ... dead now. Funny, except for ... this tired ... old body, I don't feel any different ... than when ... I first heard ... those songs." I knew exactly what she meant.

I tried to comfort her with occasional sips of water, covering her feet with the blanket and rubbing her arms. Finally I told her, "I have to go soon; our refrigerator quit cooling and the serviceman is coming to fix it this afternoon. With the party coming up, I really need to meet him." Her eyes filled with longing and I stayed another half an hour in hopes that the serviceman would be late. "I really have to go now. You take care of yourself and I'll visit you as soon as I get back from Vegas." Even though my visit exhausted her and she desperately fought to stay awake, she still didn't want me to leave, so I held her hands while she slept. Finally I decided I absolutely had to leave; she woke up as I leaned over her chair to kiss her forehead and bush her hair away from her eyes. "I'll see you soon. I love you," I whispered through my tears.

Her eyes squeezed tightly shut, she answered, "I love you too," before her lips disappeared into a muffled sobbing. I squeezed her hands one more time and placed them back on her lap before dashing out the door. I walked down the hall trying to maintain my composure while my chest felt like an exploding hand grenade.

Over the next two days we heard that she was able to stand and even walk a little. Everyone enjoyed the party, including us, and Dan left on Sunday for Las Vegas. As planned, I was to finish the party clean-up, prepare for the house guests that were scheduled to arrive shortly after our return, and join him on Tuesday.

Monday afternoon I got a call from the hospital; Ma Smith was "unresponsive". What the hell does that mean? She couldn't be wakened and her eyes didn't respond to light. Her heartbeat was strong, but she was breathing heavily. After a quick call to Dan, I began the familiar drive to the hospital. I drove with the traffic at 75 mph, but it seemed to take forever to get there. Even with the oxygen mask, Ma Smith's shoulders rose and fell with the effort of each breath. Her sallow skin and slack face still carried the tension of pain, in spite of the morphine. As I held her remarkably warm hand and tried to offer some familiar comfort, I noticed her nails were a disturbing shade of grey. After a while I gathered enough courage to ask the universe where her spirit was. She answered immediately and I felt her hovering behind me. Startled by the certainty that she was going to die, I burst into tears.

Over the next several hours, the night nurse checked her regularly and her condition remained unchanged as her precious children and grandchildren came and went. Even the nurse remembered Ma Smith from her earlier visits and mourned with us. Outside Ma's room I asked the nurse for her opinion, "Might she regain consciousness?"

A compassionate woman, her eyes softened, she hesitated, and finally she replied, "It's unlikely; she's been gone too long. There's likely to be brain damage by now."

I gradually took in the information and then asked, "How long might she stay like this?" I wasn't really eager to know, but I needed to tell Dan.

"It could be hours or days, probably not weeks. Her heart is still strong; there's no way of knowing how long she may last. "

Fighting to hold back the tears, I replied, "Well, there's never been anything wrong with her heart, in any sense of the word." As I walked away from the nurse's stand, I smiled and then laughed through my tears. I knew why she grew so tall; she needed a place large enough to house that marvelous heart.

A Brief History of the Group

The 42nd Street Irregulars began in 1986 as an outgrowth of a writing class offered at the Loft, a center for writing located in Minneapolis. The class, which focused on journal writing and family issues, was taught by Richard Solly, who encouraged several members to meet outside the class to reinforce the sharing and critiquing of their work. He then invited them to attend two workshops he was offering, where they met others interested in joining the critiquing sessions.

Solly was the model and mentor for the initial group of six, which met twice a month at a member's home. They followed the approach he had taken in class, which was based on the Loft philosophy that writers learn best from other writers and the regular practice of writing. Meetings often began with news about events and opportunities in the writing community and discussion of issues raised by the writing life. Each meeting included one or two timed writing exercises, brought by different members, whose results participants could share or not share as they chose. Often these impromptu pieces became the basis for more developed works which were brought back later for critiquing. Various members also brought their work to read aloud, or to hear it read by others. They could ask for specific advice from the group or leave themselves open to spontaneous reactions.

Essential to this activity was trust. Members were respectful of each other's unique style, personality and gifts, as well as level of development and comfort with sharing work. They listened carefully and critically, balancing sensitivity to the intensely personal nature of the creative process with the need to be candid about the quality and effectiveness of the writing. These comments were tempered, and given added weight, by the fact that everybody was equally involved in the nitty-gritty of writing, equally vulnerable, and equally in need of an authentic response.

Eventually the group gave itself a name, based on the address of its early meeting place and acknowledging its diverse membership, with a tip of the hat to a new version of Sherlock Holmes airing on PBS. Over the years, members have come and gone, the group has grown and decreased in size, and participation and productivity have waxed and waned. Some early members who sustained the group through the years, but are not represented in this collection, include Pat Simons, Sharon Skinner and Stu Tufford. Currently, with a roster of ten, only two of the original members remain. The group has survived partly because of its steady focus on honoring and supporting the writing life, and the need of those engaged in this most solitary and daunting of tasks, to find a congenial home.

The group often renews itself. Each new member provides a fresh voice and added energy. We use the first meeting of every new year to reflect on past accomplishments or disappointments and set future goals for ourselves. Occasionally when issues of group process arise—personal conflicts, maintaining a climate of respect and openness, staying on task and getting essential business done, the group has had to examine and re-dedicate itself and in some cases develop ground rules and procedures. Members take turns for a year or so to serve as the facilitator at each meeting to ensure that the agenda and guidelines are followed. As a group, or in smaller sub-groups, we have read our work at public gatherings, taken classes or workshops together and attended readings and other literary events. Every two years or so we hire a writer to lead us in a custom-tailored workshop for a day or a weekend. Past presenters include Richard Solly, Deborah Keenan, Joe Paddock and Marc Nieson.

Current membership is comprised of a rich mix of men and women, gay and straight, disabled and able-bodied, Jew, Christian and secular humanist, writers of poetry, fiction and creative non-fiction, in their 50s, 60s and now 70s. Probably what keeps us coming back, is the knowledge that this is a rare group; a welcoming, comfortable gathering of like-minded folk, all committed to the craft of writing; a safe place where you can bring almost anything, in any state of repair or disrepair, and expect to get a fair, honest and critical hearing. It is a nurturing place where fledgling works can stretch and flex their wings and learn to fly free.